Letters to My Black Sons

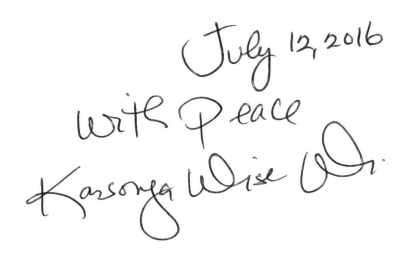

July 12, 2016

With Peace

Kasonga Wise

Letters to My Black Sons

Raising Boys in a Post-Racial America

Karsonya Wise Whitehead, Ph.D.

Apprentice House
Loyola University Maryland
Baltimore, Maryland

First Edition

Printed in the United States of America

Paperback ISBN: 978-1-62720-058-5
E-book ISBN: 978-1-62720-059-2

Design by Apprentice House

Published by Apprentice House

Apprentice House
Loyola University Maryland
4501 N. Charles Street
Baltimore, MD 21210
410.617.5265 • 410.617.2198 (fax)
www.apprenticehouse.com
info@apprenticehouse.com

Nana,
you once told me that if I ever forgot
who I was, whose I was, or why I was,
I should call because you would always remember.
You then made me promise to teach it all
—with passion, purpose, and promise—
to my boys.
And then...you made me write it down
and I haven't stopped writing since.

With my husband, Johnnie
&
For our boys, Kofi Elijah & Amir Elisha

acknowledgements

Every time I start a project, I want to move into a hole. I imagine myself digging a ditch, tossing all of my papers into it, grabbing my laptop, some snacks and a blanket, and preparing to stay there until I am done. Or I want to join a convent, move to the mountains, take a vow of silence and of poverty, and stay there until the book is finished. I get distracted so easily that if I could mail myself like Henry Box Brown to somewhere exotic but close enough to an organic market to get my daily dose of coffee and jellybeans, then I would. These are the dreams that I have though they do not fit into my reality. I write and carve my life in stiches between carpool and baseball practice; Sunday school and date nights; between family get-togethers and family game night. I write on napkins, on the backs of menus, and on my hand. Sometimes I wake up in the middle of the night and write my ideas in makeup on my vanity mirror. There are times when I show up to the page, on a perfect day with no distractions, and nothing comes out. It seems as if I cannot work unless my husband and my boys are somewhere, close by, laughing and interrupting my peace and quiet. This is my little piece of forever, this lot that I call my life, and it has been carved in noise and craziness; in daily repetition and laughter (lots and lots of laughter).

Even though there are so many people that I want to thank for loving me and for supporting me; people who understand me and who push me to be a better scholar, in this book I cannot. This book belongs to my boys—these are their letters, their experiences, and their lives spread out for the world to see. This book was written with my husband during moments of great stress and incredible happiness. Some of the pages are dog-eared. Some have food stains or smudges from tears or spilled milk. Some years my notes are very organized and I can see how their lives developed from one day to the next; other years are scattered and pages and entries are missing. I went through each of my journals—30 in total—and picked some of the letters that I felt used a long lens to view their lives. I left out the stories about potty training and late night feedings; the day when they learned how to walk and the first time they slept in their own room. I chose not to include anything that would embarrass them or make them feel exposed. I included some poetry that I wrote along the way, often in the margins of the pages. The letters are not arranged chronologically instead I have organized them around three themes: "I: Tangled Roots: shared memories" includes letters about our family—from my father's struggles growing up in the South before *Brown v Board* to my mother-in-law's battle with cancer; "II. Nurturing Masculinity: a forerunner's journey" includes letters about falling in love, the pursuit of peace, and of cultivating a spirit of integritas; and, "III. #YourLivesMatter: raising black boys, individually and collectively" includes letters about race and race relations, some of which became Opinion Editorials for The Baltimore Sun.

This book is for our boys, with our gratitude and our love. Thank you for your childhood, for choosing us to be your parents, and for always being present in our lives

January 8, 2015

preface

June 3, 2010

Dear boys:

Today you read my poetry—insights into my life that I wrote more than 20 years ago—and you had questions. I was not ready for you and for your questions about my life and my choices. I should have been more careful with my past. I should have packed those poems up, placed them in a box, and buried them upstairs in the attic next to my childhood journals. I should have written a note across the top of some of the more painful poems, begging you to succeed where I have failed in trying to burn that work. In many ways, I have kept my poetry around to inspire me, to remind me, and to encourage me to be a better writer. My poetry reminds me of who I used to be. I want my writing to leap off of the page and find a home within the heart of the reader. I want people to walk away from my work entangled in my words and my ideas I want them to take my work and use it as a lens in which they can view the world and view themselves.

I have found that I am a careless writer who composes the beginnings of masterpieces on the backs of napkins that end up being discarded. I have written and misplaced so much work that I will never be able to find again. When I was younger, I took writing for granted never working hard enough to perfect my skill. I did not think that I could make my living as a writer choosing instead to major in history. I have also spent years being careless with the work itself, never realizing that as smart and as curious as the two of you are, if I leave out pages of poetry then you would read them. "Did you really grow up in the ghetto?," you asked. "And why did you get so many spankings in dark, dusty basements? Why did grandma attack your kitchen? And what is a kitchen, anyway? And why did granddaddy send you off to college with $50 and a box full of Tide?" And on and on you went, "Who was G- and how did he break your heart? And who was R- and was he a Muslim? Why did you pledge Delta Sigma Theta? And what happened during Death Week? What did it meant that you wanted to suffer for your art and to show the world that you were real?"

You told me that you wanted to know all about me and about who I used to be before I became your Mom. I was speechless, not because I did not want to answer but because I did not know how to answer. I know who I used to be but it is so hard for me to articulate that to a 12-year old and a 10-year old who are still so very excited and happy about life. Do I talk to you about the days when the world seemed so large and my boat so small and inadequate. Do I share with you the first time I had my heart broken and how many times its broken since then? Do I talk about the days I lived in fear or the nights I cried myself to sleep? How much do I share before I begin to weigh you down from the heaviness of my memories? I tried to answer you and the words got stuck in my throat. I am not sure if you are old enough to understand what it means to have a heavy heart and how there were days when I could not even get out of bed. The world is such a dangerous and sad place and I wondered if you were ready to hear how hard I had to work to learn how to be a fighter and an advocate. I stumbled and hesitated as I tried to clearly articulate why this one simple request could not be met. I hurt you when I told you no but saying yes was never an option for me. How can I tell you who I used to be when I am still not clear about who I am?

I have been keeping journals ever since I was ten years old and at the beginning of each book, I would write:

Now I lay me down to sleep

I pray to God my soul to keep.

If I should die before I wake

Burn this diary before my mommy take(s)!

My greatest fear was that my parents would find my journals, read them, and then use the information (my pain) against me. I used to hide them all around the house and in the backyard. I tried teaching myself Russian and then started writing all of my entries in Russia. The year I spent in Kenya, I wrote everything in Swahili. I have pages and pages of whining and complaining; pining for love and wishing to be slimmer. I am not sure how I ever made it through my teenage years as I seemed to live right on the edge between despair and depression. At the same time, I knew that I had experienced a childhood where I had moments when I was incredibly happy. My parents gave us so much. I remember when we used to get teddy bears on Christmas morning that had $100 dollar bills attached to them—that was to get all of the gifts that you did not find under the tree. My father would borrow an RV and take us on road trips throughout the summer. We would drive to Pennsylvania and Delaware and stay in the parking lots of fancy hotels. Sometimes my dad would get us a room in the hotel and we would spend the day swimming and then have a fancy dinner at the hotel's restaurant. There is something about being a teenager where you seem to forget what it means to be happy.

There are days when I read my childhood journals and I tell your father that if I should die before I wake, that he is to burn my diaries before you take. I think that there are parts of my life and of my history that I do not want to share with you. I know this sounds strange coming from a historian, from someone who spends hours and hours backpacking through someone else's life, but do you really need to know everything about me? I wonder if that was what Emilie (*Notes from a Colored Girl*) told her kids to do, were they supposed to have burned her 1863-1865 diaries? Did they decide that preserving her memories was more important than respecting her wishes? Her work provides us with the answers to some very important questions that we have about the past and perhaps, this is enough to justify my work traipsing through her life (or at least I hope that it is).

I have been writing you letters ever since you were in my womb and I have documented every cold, every doctor's visit, and every issue that ever happened in your life. I had never planned to share them with you. Writing and recording your life was just a tool that I used to ground myself and to hold myself accountable. I did not want to make the same mistake twice and by writing them down, I could at least try to avoid doing so. I remember when I first told you about the letters—to my baby boys, my toddlers, my preschoolers, my tweenagers, and now, my teenagers— and the two of you sat down and read them. Amir, you laughed when you read about how you used to toddle around the room and we would run behind you to make sure that if you fell we could quickly pick you up. We knew that you were the type of baby that if you fell down, you would get comfortable, and not get up for a long time. Kofi, you were uncomfortable when you read about how hurt I was about what happened to you when you were in the first grade and the boys on the playground decided to play, "Let's Get the Black Boy." You remember that day because since you were the only black boy in your grade, you spent the entire recess running. You put down the letters and wanted to know, once again, why Daddy and I chose to send you to a predominantly white school. You have grown to love the school and you have made some good friends but you have had some hard moments. You have been bullied and ignored; overlooked and insulted but you kept getting up and going back to school. We talked about why you chose not to transfer when during a particularly difficult period in fourth grade, we were so frustrated that we were willing to move you to another school. You said (and my heart leaped at that moment), "It's my school and just like everybody else, I have a right to be there."

I asked you then if I could share my letters to you with the world. I told you that I would not do it unless the two of you agreed. You asked me for a moment and the two of you stepped into your room to confer about it. When you came back, you had one provision, you asked me not to share everything. This book is for the two of you. It is my love for you poured out onto the page. You inspire me, you challenge me, and you make me want to be better. You make me proud to call myself your mother.

Until...
Mom

Tangled Roots

shared memories

writing in the darkness

March 17, 2000

It is 3:00am in the morning and I am up sitting on the floor in the bathroom. I am sick and I have realized that I am probably pregnant. Your daddy is asleep and when I got up out of the bed, for the third time tonight, I paused for just a moment and watched him sleep. There is something very revolutionary about watching a black men finally be at peace. He will be a good father, I think, both thoughtful and kind. He will know how to love you and what to do when you cry at night. He has had some practice, as your older sister just turned nine. I remember when I first met her and I entertained the idea that I would someday be someone's mother. I laughed when I thought about it because there has never been a moment in my life when I wanted to be a mother. I do not have those kind of instincts. I barely like other people's kids and cannot imagine having one of my own. I always called them crumb snatchers and I would move away whenever I saw them coming, with runny noses and dirty hands; tear stained faces and whiney voices. I always told myself that I was not mother material and that that was ok. I really believe that the world would be a better place with far fewer people and really, I often wondered, how arrogant must a person be to want to replicate themselves. But, you are coming and you, for some reason, have chosen me to be your mother. I have decided not to wake your father as I need to have a moment with just you; a moment where we can get some things straight and agree on how this is going to go down. I am not going to change because it has taken me far too long to become the person that I am to simply give that up. My life has been spent fighting everything and everybody. I see dragons everywhere that need to be slain and it is tiring when you have been charged with the ability and the desire to fight everything and everybody. I see demons everywhere, of racism, of sexism, of classism and it is exhausting.

Your father, when we first got married last year, told me that I did not have to fight so hard anymore because he was there to fight with me when I needed it and to fight for me when I could not fight anymore. I am not comfortable with the idea of someone else fighting for me and though he is there and he is willing, I am not able. Not yet. I am a writer and my life is the canvas from which I draw my stories. You must be willing to have me present in your life with a pen and paper in one hand and your diaper bag in the other. I will try to respect your boundaries, never publishing words that will hurt you but always looking for ways to free you, even if it is only from yourself and from me. I am not perfect. I am selfish and petty; argumentative and flawed. I am probably not going to get it right and sometimes it will be because I am too tired to try. I am also a reluctant perfectionist and there will be times when I will expect you to be perfect. You will have to remind me, probably more than once, that you are not. I am a fighter and because of this, you must be born fighting. You are going to have to fight to keep my attention. You are going to have to yell if you want me to see you for who you are and not for who I think you can or should be. You are going to have to work hard and try only to learn the best of what I have to offer. I make really bad decisions and will probably forget to match your socks, to brush your hair, and to clean up your playroom. You are going to have to remind me and until you learn the words to articulate your thoughts, you must use every means possible to get my attention. I have spent too many years focusing on myself and it has become a habit, something I do without thinking about it so you will need to retrain me. And you will need to be patient with me. I have never done this before. As I sit here on the floor of the bathroom, huddled in a corner and writing my thoughts on the back of a Chinese food menu, I realize that you are already bending my life to shape your will by interrupting my sleep for the third time in one night. You know that I am tired and yet you won't be ignored. Hold on to that trait, it will help us to get through the rough patches, the moments when you begin to move from being my child to being yourself.

I got up for a moment and stood in front of the mirror and tried to imagine what you would look like. Will you get my eyes? My nose? Will you get all of the pieces of me that I don't like about myself? I want you to be special. I want you to be noticed when you walk into a room. I have never experienced this. I was not the pretty girl. I was always the smart one, the one that was overlooked, the one that boys wanted to befriend but not date. I have had crushes on boys who have never even seen me.

I am, in so many ways, invisible and it is this invisibility that drives me and keeps me from being completely satisfied with myself. I will try not to teach you this, either by word or by deed. I want you to be fully present in your own life, a change agent who is not afraid to dare to be who you are. I wonder though, my dear sweet child, how I can mother you when I have not been able to mother myself? How can I give you the tools to survive this brutal world when I have not been able to craft these tools to save myself? How can I stand up for you when my whole life has been spent trying so hard to stand up for myself? I am not perfect. I am flawed. I am pregnant. And in nine months, I will be your mother.

childhood memories

September 14, 2007

Nikki Giovanni once wrote that, "childhood remembrances are always a drag if you're black" and when other people write your story about your childhood they will never realize that in the midst of your daily struggle that you were quite happy.[1] I have come to believe, as I tell you my childhood stories, that my memories are both real and imagined. I feel like I have to preface every statement with a disclaimer that everything that I remember is real, whether it happened or not. My memories and experiences have shaped and molded me. I have found that these two things are separate because both the way that something happens and the way that I interpret and remember something happening to me are pieces of me. I make no apologies, either to my family or to my friends, for my memories or for my interpretation of them.

I. Remembering

My earliest memories are of my father sharing his stories about his childhood spent growing up in rural South Carolina; about his adventures in the military and during the Civil Rights Movement; and, about him and my Mom falling in love with each other long before they had been introduced. At night, while some kids were getting a bedtime story about green eggs and ham, my siblings and I received a history lesson about granddaddy's life before *Brown v. Board.* I remember thinking that he was just saying these things about white people to scare us and to make us straighten up and fly right because surely no one could be that cruel. On Saturday nights, my father would make us hot chocolate, stuffed with marshmallows. We would lay on the floor in our sleeping bags and he would sit in his easy chair and talk. We did not have a television so we watched our Daddy, our gifted and animated Griot who made the Movement come alive.

I felt like I was with him when he used to walk past all of the white schools to get to his all-black one-room classroom. I used to feel the heat when he would describe the big black cast iron stove that set in the middle of the classroom burning wood throughout the winter to keep the room warm. I used to squint when he would talk about how everyone had to move to one side of the classroom in the afternoon so that they could use the sunlight to see their books. I used to shiver when he would talk about how he only had one coat and two pair of shoes—one for everyday and one pair for Sunday church. He used to wear his shoes until he got holes in the bottom and then he would put in a cardboard strip and wear them a little bit longer. He told us how he used to wake up hungry and spend the day thinking about food. There was just enough food to keep him from starving but not enough to make him feel full. My father shared stories about his life and how difficult it was growing up black and poor and male in the South. He believed, as did my grandmother, that the only thing that could save him from a lifetime of poverty and malnutrition was either a good education or the military. My father chose education and would study every night and make promises to himself along the way, "If I get an A on the chemistry test, then I'm going to buy myself a honey bun." He kept a secret ledger with a balance sheet and every time he made an "A," he would pay himself a quarter. He would pay himself when he had to clean the outhouse or when he gave his sister the last slice of bread or when he had to pick cotton or sweep the sand out of the house. It became a game of how much could he pay himself not to complain or cry out or just stop believing that life would ever change. He promised himself that as soon as he made it, the first thing he was going to do was pay himself and go and get everything he always dreamed about in his ledger.

II. Discovering

My favorite story, and the only one that my parents would tell together, is about how they met and fell in love. They used to finish each other sentences and laugh out loud, as the details started to change once they got older. My father fell in love with my mother when he was 13 years old. Their churches used to host a joint picnic where all of the families would come together and worship. My mother was a city girl. Her mother (my Nana) was one of the few black nurses in South Carolina and her father (my Dee Dee) worked for the railway. They used to come to the picnic in a car, one of the few families that owned one. There were eight of them, my father remembers because he counted all the kids as they got out. My mother was the last one out and he said that he knows this because she swung her legs out first and he thought it was odd that her knees were shining. He said that he remembered that the day was slightly overcast because he heard it was going to rain and he had thought about not coming. "She smiled," he used to say as he eyes looked away for just a moment, "and it was like the sun had finally come out." That summer my father had finally saved enough money to buy a white suit. He had worked everyday after school and had saved every single penny. He felt like a man on the day he bought that suit home in a paper bag.

My mother said she saw him out the corner of her eye. He fascinated her because she had never seen a black boy in an oversized starched white suit with the cuffs and the sleeves rolled up. She remembers that he had on white shoes and white socks as well. "He did not sit with the other kids," she said, "he sat with the men and he talked to them like he was one of them." My mother sat with her sisters; close enough to pretend as if she was not listening to him. She thought he was smart and wanted to say something to him but back then, good girls never spoke to boys first. My father did not speak either. He just watched her whenever she laughed or walked around. He said his heart dropped when all eight kids piled back into the car. Their father did not say a word, he just got up and all of them started to move. He said they looked happy and healthy, like they ate one day at a time never worrying about whether they would eat tomorrow.

He did not see her again for an entire year. On the eve of the annual picnic, he took his suit out of the back of the closest—he had hid it there so that he would not be tempted to wear it—and laid it across his chair. It fit him this summer and like before, he spent the whole afternoon sitting with the men and watching her whenever she moved. She spent the day trying to figure out whether my father was wearing a new suit or the same suit. And if it was the same suit, why was it so white? It looked like he had not worn it at all; in fact, he had not. The summer before (after he met her), he had decided that he wanted to have one nice thing for the picnic so he saved the suit. When my mom was getting ready to leave, he walked over to and introduced himself. She said he did not smile though he said he could not remember doing anything but that.

When she saw him the next summer, she said her heart leaped. The white suit, the one that he had worn both times she saw him, was now a little too small. She could see his wrists and his ankles.

He was 16 and she was 14. He talked to her this time and they sat together at the picnic. He was not thinking of marriage or commitment. He just wanted to talk to the pretty brown girl with the shiny knees. They do not remember what they talked about it, something about the future, schoolwork, traveling, and their parents. They both wanted out of South Carolina and had dreams of going to school up North. My father joined the military at 18 and though he never saw my mother at another picnic, he said he used to dream about her and tell all of his bunkmates that when he got home, he was going to find her and marry her. Four years later, when he arrived at her door, my mother was shocked when he simply announced that he was ready to get married and he was ready to get married to her. She was 20 years old and was dating a law student from Boston. They never told me how he won her heart (some secrets really should be just between lovers) just that he did and they were married within the next year. He told that he would take her away from all of this—the racism, the South, the struggle—and they would start over with a clean slate.

III. Assembling

They settled in Washington, DC and my father worked at a gas station during the day and attended college at night. I know that he worked and went to school when I was child but I do not have any memory that does not include him. He was always there, every trip or family night or Parent Teacher Conference. He showed up each and every time. I remember once when my teacher started talking to me at a Parent Teacher Conference. My mother had stepped out to check on my sister and I was standing there by myself. My teacher looked down at me and started telling me everything that I needed to change to be a better student. I remember that my hands started shaking, as they usually do when I get upset, and right before I said anything my father suddenly appeared, took my hand, and begin to answer the teacher in my defense. He told me that night that he was my first line of defense, when I am wrong he would be the first person to correct me and when I was right, he would be the first to defend me. He was like a superhero to me and there were days when I felt like I had my own special bat signal that I could use whenever I felt afraid or alone. My father worked hard so that my childhood memories would not be a drag. I remember that I was never hungry, I never thought about food, or wore shoes lined with cardboard. I never used an outhouse or had to boil water to take a shower. I never had a ledger because I had my daddy. I remember summer vacations, hot chocolate, and stories about the Movement. I remember laying on my daddy's shoulder and always feeling like it was put there just for me.

For years, I wondered about how my father changed his economic situation. I now believe that it was a combination of things. The first is that he enlisted in the military and by doing so, he received a monthly income, healthcare, and a housing allowance, which allowed him to save a large portion of his pay. Next, my father pursued educated and was committed to receiving a college degree and becoming a minister. He later earned both his Master's Degree and his Doctorate of Ministry. Additionally, my mother supported my father's dreams and though she could not "see" them, she believed that they were real and attainable. She was a stay at home mom and she did everything she could to ensure that our home was a place of peace and love and stability. Next, and often overlooked, is that my father had multiple opportunities to help him along the way. He had an uncanny ability to predict those moments when opportunity and talent would coalesce. Some of his friends called it the "Wise luck," I call it being attuned to your talents and always being ready to use them. Finally, my father has grit, which is hard to describe and even harder to quantify. He has that unique ability to focus on a goal and finish it. He can will himself to the finish line despite whatever obstacles might be in his path. He is amazing. He has told me and has shown me how important it is to have your history be a stepping-stone for your destiny. It should not hold you back rather it should be seen as a necessary step that will propel you to the next level.

IV. Accepting

My father carved out a path for me to follow and left both his footprints and breadcrumbs to guide me through. He has told me that the path that has been carved for me was designed just for me; therefore, I am not in a race. Everything that is for me is for me alone. It is a journey and though there are times that I feel that I have been walking for a long time, I am still on the path and am a long way from home. My memories, both real and imagined, are my guideposts that I am using (just like my daddy's footprints and breadcrumbs) to guide me back home. My father, your grand-father, has trained me well so I understand that as I make my way through I need to step hard and leave large breadcrumbs for you to follow. My memories, my stories, have now been given to you, treat them well.

shared work

May 30, 2005

You once asked me, as I was tucking you into bed, what my favorite thing was about being your mommy. I told you that I had two favorite parts, the first was watching you and your baby brother find your way in the world and the second was watching you with your daddy. Tonight, as he was helping you to get dressed for my parent's anniversary dinner, you wanted to know what Mommy was giving them for their special day. You thought that it was strange that I did not have a gift and that all I kept talking about was the poem. Daddy laughed and told you that I was a writer and that the only gifts I ever gave, the ones that really mattered to me, were the ones that had been carved by me with my pencil onto my paper. You ran into your room, grabbed your crayons and a piece of paper and said, "Me too! I got to make Pop-Pop's gift before we go." I laughed then but I cried later that night when as I finished reading my poem, you stood up and read yours, as well.

As Two Become One
(for Mom & Dad, ©2005)

It has been noted that the two of you have learned
what matters most
You have learned about the renewing of love
seeking new grounds to discover and new heights to climb
You alone know how your marriage is a journey
And how precious your time together, really is
How anchoring. How soothing. How comfortable.
You, as a couple, who have been together a long time,
 and have become stitched quilt-like into one another.

You two have become one,
 knowing full well that this journey, your shared life, was not easy.
But, you did it. And in doing it, you have enlightened the way.
You've done it mostly for yourselves but partly for us too...
You have grown in your love
Remained anchored and real and true
35 years of a marriage well lived
You have shown us what real love
 —through struggle and sacrifice—looks like.
We are anchored in the solidness of you
We have learned your childhood stories and will tell them well

Your love is bonded, confirmed, and deep-rooted!
There are times when we watch you
 and we bear witness to the exactness of your love
 and the depth of your joy and pleasure with and in one another

You have been through many storms together.
Anchoring yourselves in Christ and holding tight to one another.

You have weathered and have grown wise from the experience.
You have shown us what it means to lay down who you are
and pick up who you want to be together.

You (two) are a blessing.
You are (after 45 years) at peace and in love
Confirmed. Real. Committed. & Still together.

Heres a Kiss
(Kofi Whitehead, ©2005)

PopPop and Granma
from me Kofi to you
I love you!!!
happy day
Thank You for being good to me
Heres a kiss

shifting perspectives

June 1, 2011

I stood at your door tonight as you were reading one of my poems to your brother. At the end, you started laughing and said, "Mommy wrote this for grandma but doesn't this sound just like her?" I realized then that I had become my mother. I was a 41-year old Griot and I was responsible for helping to shape the ways in which you see yourself and the world. Sometimes, it is hard being your mother because (and I suspected this a long time ago), you and your brother are much smarter than I was at your age. You are technologically savvy and you move with a confidence that belies your age. You have been places that I, as a child, had only dreamed about. I have tried so hard to be a good mommy and I have failed more times than I would like to admit. I have tried to remember to apologize when I got it wrong and to (gently) remind you when I got it right. I know that I am not perfect. There will come a day when you and your brother will approach me and want to have that conversation—the one where you demand answers about some of the decisions I made when you were children and explanations about situations where your feelings were hurt or your expectations were not met—the same one that I had with my parents when I returned home from Kenya. My hope is that when

I tell you that I did the best that I could do and that I tried with only the purest of intentions, that that will be enough to help to satisfy your curiosity and to help you to forgive me.

Permutations
(for Mom, ©1988)

at 40-something years old
my mother's hair is in state of evolution

after years of pulling it out when she was worried
and jerry-curling it when she wasn't

after afroing it doing the 60s revolution
and perming it during the 70s pacification

without any further assistance from her
my mother's hair is growing gray and growing kinky

its in a state of judgment not denial

every wrong that i have ever done, thought or said
can be measured by the gray hairs on my mother's head

every time i have stayed out late forgetting to call
can be measured by the kinkiness of not just one strand but all

my mother's hair is in a state of revolution

happening now when its ok to be self-confident and self-true
when we, as human beings, see being different as being you

taking place in a world where you now get respect for having aged
my mother her spirit her hair so free and now uncaged

at 40-something years young
my mother's hair is in a state of transformation

a life force a pattern a blueprint for future growth
a mane of crowning glory that would make any soul sister boast

its growing its sprouting like its life has just begun
at a time when we all figured my mother's growth was done

finally becoming everything i had always hoped she would be
wild and untamed emancipated and free

finally becoming my father's daughter

March 5, 2013

My editor just called and wanted to know if I had made a decision about what name I was planning to use on the front of my book (*Notes from a Colored Girl*). He said that since I had so many of them (he knows this because he has used Google to look them all up), I had to make a choice about how I wanted to be introduced to the world. He believes (as I do) that my book will travel to places that I will not go and interact and impact the lives of people who I will never meet. He said I had to make a decision about who I wanted to be. You know that I have spent the last five years of my life writing the Emilie book, pouring everything that I had into it. She became real to us, accompanying us on every family vacation. She was there when you graduated from Lower School and was present when we went on family vacations. You once told me (perhaps in frustration) that you would be glad when the book was done so that she could leave our lives and you could have your mommy back. And now that she is done and is on the verge of leaving us, what name should I put on my book, our book?

My name on that book will be all that people have that connects Emilie to me. I spent a lot of time thinking about this question and trying to make a very difficult decision. When I shared it with you and your brother, you laughed and said, "Your name? Mommy, that's an easy one." As you said, "Karsonya" and Amir said, "Kaye" and Daddy laughed and said, "Akilah" —you began to understand my dilemma. It may seem simple on the surface but for someone who has spent a lifetime naming and renaming herself, it was not an easy decision. I suppose, like so many other things in my life, I could blame my parents, since I came into the world and lived for the first week of my life without a name. It took me a long time to recognize and understand why names are important and how they connect us to ourselves.

I. Kofi Elijah

When we first found out that we were pregnant with you, your father and I thought long and hard about what we were going to name you. We wanted to give you a name that you could grow into and that you could someday claim as your own. I remember we used to watch Kofi Annan on television and I was always so impressed by the ways in which he spoke to the problems of the world. He was from Ghana and was the head of the United Nations. When we researched his name we found out that it meant "Born on a Friday" and since you were due on Friday, January 12 then the decision was made. Your daddy wanted your middle name to be Elijah, a Hebrew name which means "Jehovah is God." He was an Old Testament prophet and we believed that like Kofi and Elijah, you would be called upon to speak to and lead many nations.

I had a difficult pregnancy. You did not like being in the womb and I did not like having to deal with your discomfort. I went into pre-term labor right after our 24th week together. I was scared and my doctor warned me that I had a long road ahead of me and that I had to be confined to my bed until after my 38th week. I cried because I was television producer and I could not imagine not being able to finish my work, to make (what I thought) were major contributions to the world. I remember when I was lying in the hospital bed, my doctor had stepped out for a moment and your daddy had gone to try and call his parents, and I placed my hands on my stomach. "Kofi," I said (and this was the first time that I called you by your name), "I need you to work with me. We have four months to go and you cannot come out until you are ready. Here's the deal, you do your part and stay in there and I will do my part and stay in bed." As the weeks gave into months and I was rushed back and forth to the hospital every single week, I realized then that you were your own person and if I could not control your behavior in the womb then surely I would not be able to control you once you arrived. I made the decision not to try. On January 11, one day before you were due (and we had carefully counted and celebrated everyday), my doctor noticed that every time I had a contraction, your heart rate dropped. She told me that it was time to go in and get you. I hesitated because it was Thursday night. It was 11:30 and I asked the doctor, much to my chagrin, if there was anyway that we could wait until 12 am. Your name is Kofi and I did not want you to have a lifetime of explaining your name. I think that she thought that I was delirious and looking back, I probably was.

Your name is Kofi–you have embraced both it and your story. When you were in first grade, you came home and told us that your classmates were mispronouncing your name. They were calling you "Coffee" and "Caw-fee." You said that you spent the entire day correcting them because your name was the first gift ever given to you by your parents and they had to call you what you wanted to be called.

II. Amir Elisha

On your brother's one-year birthday, right after he blew out the candles, he looked around the room and announced for all to hear that he had wished for a baby brother. He then wanted to know how he could get one. I remember when we found out two days later that we were going to have you, he clapped and clapped and said, "I got what I wanted! I got what I wanted." Choosing your middle name was easy, just like my pregnancy. You were going to be Elisha, the prophet who worked with Elijah and who asked for and received a double portion of his blessing. I worked straight through the pregnancy, sometimes forgetting that you were there. Kofi would come in at night and tell you all about his day. He would lay his head on my stomach and shout at you. Since we could not decide on a first name, we just called you Baby Boy. He would play a game with you where he would pat my stomach and wait for you to kick and then he would pat another section and wait for you to kick there. Every night, the two of you would pat and kick until bedtime. I remember one night when no matter where Kofi patted, you kicked on the opposite side and he could not understand why you did not follow him. I was happy about that because I knew that if you were going to be a part of the Whiteheads then you had to be able to make your own decisions. We are a loud family and there is no space for someone who cannot speak up and advocate for himself. It was not until we were hospital and you were getting ready to be born that Daddy finally said, "Amir Elisha." When I looked at him, he said that if anything were to happen to me, he wanted me to know that our son was going to have the name that I really wanted him to have. Amir is both a Hebrew name meaning "powerful and proclaimed" and a Persian name meaning "King." Elisha means "my God is salvation." You were born with a big name and I have watched as you have grown into a young prince and are on your way to being a King. You are headstrong and stubborn; clear about what you want and not afraid to challenge authority. You are the one who has changed me the most because you are so much like me. I have worked on becoming a better person so that the road you are traveling—the one that will take you back to yourself—is one that I can tell you about from personal experience.

III. Karsonya Eugenia

When grandma was pregnant with me, her aunts told her and my father that they could tell by the way that she was carrying me that I was going to be a boy. When my father first heard this, he held on to it and decided right then to call me Carson Eugene Jr. It never even occurred to my parents to choose a girl's name because in their eyes, there was no need. When I showed up, they were not prepared so for the first week of my life, I was simply called "Baby Girl Wise." My mother laughed when she told me that when my father first told her my name, she initially disliked it. "It's too big for a girl," she complained. "She'll grow into it," my father replied. "But why that name," my mother wanted to know, "Why not Dorothy after my mother or Maria after yours?" "Because she is not a Dorothy or a Maria. She is unique. Special. And she needs her own name," he replied. "But," my mother continued, "she's named after you, which probably means that she is going to be a lot like you." My father, according to my mother, simply picked me up, whispered something in my ear, and carried me over to the window. She thinks that he whispered my name, I suspect that he probably whispered his.

I am my father's daughter. I always have been. Yet I have always struggled with my name. It *was* too big and awkward and people constantly mispronounced it. I was in elementary school when I first decided to change my name. It was my first act of resistance. I remember the day that I gathered up my courage and asked my father if I could change my name. He looked at me for a long time and then said, "You can change your name to anything you like and I will respect it. I will call you what you want to be called. Your name, even though I love it, is yours to keep or change."

IV. Renaming

So, in elementary school, right after I became the first girl captain of the safety patrol, I became "Sonia"–bold and brave. I felt empowered and in control because I had named myself. In middle school, I switched to "Cassandra" which I felt was a better name for a budding young musician. I joined a band in sixth grade and even though all we did was beat on our desks during class, we swore that we were making real music. I used to wear my daddy's shirts to school, roll up my jeans at the bottom, and wear white tennis shoes without any socks. By the time I reached 12th grade, I was "So-So," living a dual existence as a cheerleader and the editor of the school newspaper. I had been invisible for three years, so when I became a cheerleader and became popular, I felt I needed a new name to go with my new life. I learned a difficult lesson that year, that my name (like my father once told me) does not define me.

I entered college as "Karsonya" and quickly became the president of my first year class. I was serious and studious and wanted to become the next Barbara Jordan. Along the way, I became Angela Davis instead. I read *Malcolm X*, *Assata Shakur*, and the *Little Red Book*. I pledged Delta Sigma Theta, started growing dreadlocks, and changed my name to "Akilah Fatima."

It never even occurred to me that people would not call me by what I wanted to be called. My parents did and if they could call me "Sonia," "Cassandra," "So-So," or "Akilah," then everyone else could as well. And just about everyone did, because that was who

I was and what I had chosen to be called. In my last year of school, I traveled to Nairobi, Kenya and lived for a while with a Massai family. Before I left the country, they inducted me into their family, giving me both a traditional Massai apron and a family name. I was "Kipkembe," which meant "happy one." After the ceremony, I sat with my Massai mother and laughed as I told her that I already had far too many names and that I really did not need another one. She shook her head and said, "You don't have too many names, you have one name and that it is the one given to you at birth by your parents." All the rest of them, were mine to use or not, but my name, the one that my father may have whispered in my ear, was the first gift that my parents had ever given me.

I thought long and hard about what she said and about how important it was for me to finally know and claim not just my name but also my life and my family history. I thought about my father and the conversation that we had right before I left for the continent. We went out for a short hike and he shared with me that his dream had always been to go to Africa and since he could not go then I was going to go for both of us. He said that when our ancestors first arrived in America, they came as slaves, in chains and bound one to the other. They went forward without knowing what lay ahead of them. They were survivors and as such, we are survivors. It is something that comes as natural to us as breathing and being. We are descendants from people that chose to survive. "Since I can't go to Africa," he said very quietly, "I am sending them the next best thing. I am sending them you because you are my daughter and where you go, I am there with you."

V. Acceptance

I thought about all of this when your father and I very thoughtfully and very carefully selected your names. You are our children but the decision about who you are going to be, is yours alone. Everywhere that you go, you take us with you and that is not simply because of your name but because of who you are and what we have poured into you. You are our diamonds and we have molded and shaped you; sparked your genius; and are prepared, to one day set you free to set the world on fire. I am Karsonya Eugenia, my father's daughter and you are my children. It is that name—the one that is both his and mine, the first gift that I have ever received—that will go on the cover of all of my books. It is my name and it is a part of who I am and who I have chosen to be. My hope is that when you finally make the choice about who you are and who you want to be that your names—our first gift—will be anchors to ground you, rutters to direct you, and sails that set you free.

remembered sacrifices

October 15, 2013

I. Remembering Reds

I was born in South Carolina. My father grew up in Lexington County on a farm with an outhouse, miles of land, and a lake that sat at the bottom of the hill at the edge of their property. He picked cotton over the summer, taking long rest breaks to read his book, one chapter at a time. He had one suit, white. When he bought it, his mother, my dear sweet grandmother Marie, told him that it was too long so she made him roll up both the pant legs and the sleeves. Every year, he would roll it down until the year that he was able to see both his ankles and his wrists. My grandmother had a mane of blazing red hair and a personality that was almost too big to capture. She seemed to always be in motion, even when she was standing still. She was a big woman but she walked very lightly, almost as if she was gliding across the floor. I used to go fishing with her though I knew she did not like to take me. I talked too much and had too many questions. She liked to just sit, in silence, and wait for something to happen. "Black people," she used to say, "have been waiting all their lives for something good to happen. If they can wait for freedom to come, then surely I can wait on some fish to bite."

She used to wear an old straw hat, a jersey dress, and black flip-flops. She used to like to chew on a stalk of grass. She was a pretty woman, a Southern girl. I remember when she would take me into town in her blue car. She would let down all of the windows and drive really fast because the car did not have central air. "Sometimes," she said as she stared wistfully out the window, "you got to drive fast to meet the change that you are waiting to come." I would just laugh, not because I understood but because I did not. I thought she was joking because when she would say things like that, she would look over at me, wink her eye, and start laughing. She had a quiet laugh where her whole body shook but she barely made a sound. She had dimples and freckles and moles. She was Sunday morning and Thursday afternoons all rolled up in one person. She made me feel good and special. She told me that I could be anything I wanted to be and even more than that if I put my mind to it. "You're a black woman," she shouted as we walked through the woods on the way to the pond, "and we've been holding up our little piece of the world for a long time. If we can hold that up for so long with so little then surely you can do your part. You can go and see the world, and then you can change it. You come from a long line of women who knew what it meant to work for change." My grandma Reds, she was something else and even if she never said it, she was a feminist.

II. Understanding Nana

My grandma Nana, my mother's mother was also a feminist. She was the yin to Reds' yang. Reds was country and real. She was sandy floors and screen doors. She was about picking cotton and catching fish. She moved fast but took life slow because in her words, it was too darn hot to move too fast. Nana was different. She was an educated city girl. She was white gloves and refined hats; leather purses and white stockings; she was classy and prim. She wore cotton in the Spring, linen in the Summer, and worsted wool during the Winter. She was absolutely flawless at all times. She grew up in Ola, South Carolina and went on to attend a private all-girls boarding school. She graduated at the top of her class and went on to become one of the few black nurses in South Carolina.

I remember when I used to go and visit her and she would make me get dressed to come to the breakfast table, telling me that I had no idea who might show up and I needed to be ready. She used to make me read out loud to her because I had a pretty voice and I needed to be ready in case I ever spoke before the president or before her pastor. She gave me the first items for my trousseau and then told me to go out and see the world before I got married. "I married your Dee-Dee before I got a chance to see the world," she used to tell me, "and now, eight kids later, my world is right here in Columbia." She would tell me that she was blessed and that this was the life that she had chosen; but, if she could do it again, she would see the world first. "Marriage is a blessing and I love being a married woman," she said, "but the world is so big and once you have kids, it is hard to imagine going beyond what you can see."

I went and visited her before I left to spend a year in Kenya. I sat at the table with her and talked on and on about what I was planning to do once I got there. She just listened with tears rolling down her face and then said, "You're going to get there and I'm going with you." She said that I had to be more than a candle but less than a forest fire. She explained that since candles burned out and forest fires raged out of control, I had to make sure that I neither burned out nor went out of control. I needed to light the way but remain rooted in who I was and whose I was. She said, "You have to write everything down, even the little things, because I want to hear all about it when you come back to me." She used to tell me about Harriet Tubman, Coretta Scott King, and her grandmother. "Black women," she would explain, "are powerful beyond measure. We stand as a veil of protection between the world and our families. I have taught you how to stand and you must teach your children how to do it as well. We must be women who will not sit in the face of danger but will stand and like David, we will run to meet our challenges. We will lean into those spaces and claim them as our own. Remember that. And if you ever forget who you are, whose you are, and why you are, call me because I will never forget." She was smart and funny and real.

III. Together

When I told grandma Reds that I was going to Africa she took me with her to pick cotton. I had only picked cotton once before on my tenth birthday. She told me that I could keep all the money that I earned that day. I picked cotton from sunup to sundown and I believe I made about $2.50 but for a ten-year old during the 70s, that felt like a lot of money. When we picked cotton this day, I remember how hot I was and how hard it was to keep my back bent over for long stretches of time. My hands were getting scratched as I worked hard to pull all of the cotton off. I was drenched in sweat before 10:00am and we still had to rest of the day to work. I complained once and she stood up and looked at me for a long time. "You're a Anderson," she quietly said, "and Andersons don't complain. We move mountains because we can and we finish every job that we start." She then turned and worked without saying another word to me for the rest of the day. I was crying by the end and when they weighed my bag and gave me three dollars, I was indignant. I could not believe that I had worked hard all day for pennies. When we got in the car and sat drinking our cold pops, she told me that I was at the beginning of a journey that was going to change my life. She talked about our family legacy and how enslavement and bondage were a part of our history. We were the children of people who chose to survive. She told me to think about the women who were taken from Africa and put on a ship without having any idea of where they were going and then they had to make a decision to survive. She said that I could not go back to the continent unless I understood that I was a descendant of people (of women) who had chosen to survive. I had to remember that though Africa was a part of my heritage, America—with all of her imperfections—was my home. She then said, "Go wherever the adventure takes you and when it is over, remember to come back home." She hugged me for a long time that day and kept telling me to remember.

And I did. I remembered what they both said when I was backpacking in Nairobi and when I was climbing mountains in Tanzania; when I was visiting churches in Ethiopia or sitting in the hot springs in Wondo Genet. I remembered their teachings when I was working with kiosk women and when I was teaching young girls how read. I ran to meet my challenges while I was on the continent and remembered often that Africa, beautiful and peaceful as it was, was not my home. Reds passed away before you had a chance to meet her. She never knew that her favorite wild child, her travel bug and fishing partner, had gotten married and had become somebody's mommy. She always told me not to forget and I have spent hours trying to share all of her stories with you. I believe, like she once told me, that if your stories are being told then your life and your legacy continue.

You grew up with Nana and you had a chance to learn about her life and to hear her stories from her perspective. She had a chance to teach you, to love you, to support you, and to tell you all about who you are destined to become. She said that you had genius flowing through you and that you were the ones that our family had been waiting for. They are both gone now but their spirits and their stories live on through you. You are the grandchildren of two women who chose to survive and this is your legacy and it is a part of who you are.

I asked for your help when I was writing Nana's tribute because I was too close to be able see the richness and the fullness of her life. The two of you sat with me, you held me hands, and cried with me. You reminded me of who she was and everything she had always wanted to become. You told me that I was her granddaughter and that I had to honor her so that the world would know who she was. You said that even though she had run on ahead to see how the end was going to be, I had to stay in this moment and bear witness to her life. You could not understand why I could not stop crying. It was because the two of you sounded just like my Nana and my Reds—honoring my loss but reminding me of the work that I had to do. If they could hold their little piece of the world up for so long with so little, then surely I could go forward and make them proud.

Remembering Nana
(for Dorothy Bamberg, ©2013)

I stand here today as someone who loved, appreciated, admired and respected Dorothy Best Griffin Bamberg—my Nana.
I stand here today to remember a woman who defined class and grace, honesty and dignity, life and love
a woman who blazed trails and lit up a room simply by walking into it.
I stand here today to stand still for just a moment to take stock of a life that was well lived; a blueprint for future generations; a snapshot of her life from my eyes.

She was a genuine visionary
A carrier of the human spirit
A chronicler of this side of life
She was molded and sculpted
Her life imprinted onto the roots of our hearts
She was planted among us
Artfully seeded in the soil of South Carolina to illuminate our texts,
to shepherd our prayers,
to spiritualize our commitments,
and to help us to heal the holes in our hearts.

How do you thank someone who has spent her entire life
working to create things that are designed to make us better,
to make us think about who we are,
to challenge us to go farther than we ever thought possible
someone   who worked so hard on our behalf
and who redefined
what it meant to be a woman: a wife, a mother, a grandmother, a great grandmother, a sister, a friend...
thereby giving the universe an insight into
what it means to sacrifice

Women, like Dr. Dorothy Bamberg,
They are oak trees having endured the hurricanes of racism,
the volcanoes of sexism,
and the earthquakes that come
from growing up and being black and female and poor in America

If there was a time to pray
Then Nana was somewhere kneeling
If there was a time to work

Then Nana was somewhere getting her hands dirty
If there was someone somewhere who needed to be saved
Or who needed a helping hand or a kind word
Then Nana, without question without hesitation, was right there
And if there was a time to lead
Then Nana naturally and gracefully rose to the occasion

We must and should read her life differently
Women like Dot must be held to a different standard
Because they know how to look and to reach beyond
My nana possessed a deep-rooted joy
When she laughed she did so with every fiber of her being
It was like sunshine had entered a room and sat down right next
to her

We have to read her life differently
She was cut from a different mold
Good people like her really cannot be judged like the rest of us

She made music, pointed out the truth,
and took her time to hear your voices
Her interior is tree-lined, South Carolina wheat grass, mountainous
She instilled questions and common sense
Urged mighty thoughts and lively expectations
She was an example of discipline and hard work
She made life seem exciting and new challenging and real
She was like a quiet space
In the midst of a world full of noise and chaos and confusion

How do we celebrate the life of someone who created music with
her words
Showered love on her family and friends,

Someone who had a deeper calling?

How do we go forward with half a heart?

What is the message in her transition from body to spirit to the quiet recesses of our minds?

What should we take from her passing?

And what should we say when folks try to consul us with empty words, folks who don't know or understand what we have truly lost?

We tell them that we are celebrating someone
  who interpreted beauty and loved life
Someone who was patient with people and didn't mind them calling her
Dorothy Bamberg saw genius in her children
  & nurtured genius in her grandchildren

She saw possibilities when others saw problems
She saw potential when others saw predicaments

We tell them how her voice was majestic and magnetic
And of how she spoke in rhythms, song, and spirited trumpets

We tell them that she was unstoppable and completely unforgettable
  and when she entered a space—It was never the same again

We tell them that we are celebrating the wisdom of her life

The quietness of her spirit
The greatness of her love

We remember all of who she was
  and commit to learning from her mistakes,
  and growing from her lessons.

We must be the ones who remember her.
And now that we are at this moment,
let us not forget that she was light and hope and beauty and love
Let us always remember that she confirmed life
Let us not neglect to tell the world that she confirmed us
Let us commit to passing her name on to every generation
Dorothy Best Griffin Bamberg—was one of the greats
Her name and her contributions   will never ever be forgotten

the cancer journals: beginnings[2]

April 18, 2013

For the past couple of days, I have been thinking about how hard it is to be a grown up. You have so much to worry about and so much to do. It is almost as if you are running a race and just when you think you are near the finish line, someone moves it. My life is now an endless stream of moving finish lines. I feel old today; not because of my age but because I am tired of not being able to see the end. (I keep wanting to put down my load and run ahead, slightly beyond where the end is going to be.) I have been thinking a lot about death today; maybe it is because my grey hair is starting to come back or maybe it is because cancer has finally come back to my circle of my life. I never used to think about cancer and about what it does to the body or how it affects your spirit.

Eleven years ago, your great-grandfather died of prostate cancer and though I did not bear witness to his daily struggle; I do know that he fought it with everything that he had. My grandfather spent the greater part of his life laying railroad tracks in the South that led to places in the North that he would never have a chance to visit. He was over six feet tall; taller than my daddy and every other man that I knew. I used to beg him to pick me up because I thought if he held me up, I could actually touch the clouds. He used to come out in the yard when we played and his shadow would darken everything and everybody. I remember his laugh, which sounded like music and made me think of sunshine. He used to kneel in front of me (this was long before the arthritis made it hard for him to do this) and give me hugs and kiss my nose. He had these huge hands. I remember that when I was a little girl, he used to grab both of my hands in one of his and help me get across the room. I have a picture of him before he got sick and, like every picture I have with him, I am holding his hands. I also remember kissing his hands when the arthritis started to set in and he could not bend them anymore.

He was a fighter and he fought that cancer for two years. When he first got sick, the hospice workers told us that he only had a few weeks to live and then, those weeks stretched into months and then into years. In my mind, I saw him as a soldier using his hands, his bible, his faith, and his laughter to battle back the cancer and keep it at bay. When we saw him for the last time—when the cancer had taken just about everything he had to give—he asked if you could sing him his favorite song. Your Daddy held you up as you sang "Jesus Loves Me This I Know." My grandfather leaned back into his pillows and smiled, as the tears ran down his face. I remember that I cried when you held out his hand and my grandfather, very slowly, lifted his hand, and grabbed it. It was a full circle moment and though you do not remember this and my grandfather has moved on, I remember and that image still makes me smile and cry.

You are now twelve and cancer, like an unwelcome guest, has come back into our lives again. Time has passed, I have gotten older (even more cynical) and I still feel as devastated and shocked and confused as I did when I first found out about my grandfather. When I received the news about my grandfather, I remember going to the library and checking out every book that I could find about prostate cancer and after reading through all of them, I sat there feeling overwhelmed and confused. I felt the same way, two months ago when we found out that your grandmother (your daddy's mother) has lung cancer. I keep telling myself that times have changed, medicine has gotten better, and the field has been revolutionized; but, in so many ways, it has not. There is still no cure for terminal cancer and there is nothing worse than having a doctor tell you that there is nothing that can be done to cure the person that you love. Nothing. At all. In less than two months after receiving the diagnosis, your grandmother's voice has been reduced to a whisper and she moans in pain whenever we touch her. She has moved from being a vibrant healthy person to being bedridden in less than sixty days.

I first met your grandmother thirteen years ago and back then she seemed larger than life. Fearless. Unafraid. She would enter a room and the air would shift just a bit. You could feel the energy radiating off of her. Pure power. It took a while for her to like me and for us to be ok with one another. In retrospect, I realize that it was hard work trying to get two big personalities to coexist in the same space, at the same time. It was after I had you that I think my personality shrunk just a bit in her presence. I was a young mother and a young wife, and I was trying to juggle every ball that I had and still remain who I was. It was too tiring to fight to be heard in her presence, I just listened. And over time, the listening became easier. I learned to take a book to her house so that I could read whenever the visits started to overwhelm me. I think that was when I started to grow up and realize that being an adult meant that I did not always have to remind people of who I was and what I believed in…sometimes just being there was enough.

I am afraid for your grandmother. Although I am a Christian (and so is she) and I believe that there is spiritual life after this physical death, I am still afraid. I keep asking myself over and over again whether I am afraid of death or afraid of dying. I know about death (and really, who does not) and it is actually hard to be afraid of something that comes as a thief in the night. I am actually prepared for death as I feel like it is only a phone call away. Much like my parents did when I was young, I now jump when the phone rings between 12a and 5a in the morning and I am a little nervous when my parents tell me that they are not feeling well or when my Nana makes another trip to the ER. I remember the exact moment of every phone call that I have ever received where someone told me that someone I loved had died. It is not my own death that scares me, it is the impending death of those I love that keeps me awake at night.

It is the dying that scares me, bothers me, and makes me feel unsettled. It is the constant chipping away that cancer does to your spirit and your body that unnerves me. There are only a few things in this world that only belong to you and have always only belonged only to you. One of those things is your body, it is yours: every pound lost or gained, every scar, every deformity or mishap, every broken nail and grey hair and wrinkle, all yours. Your body is a roadmap that perfectly outlines your life journey and it is always working with you and never against you...except when you get a terminal illness, like cancer. As I watch her struggle, it is almost as if her body has turned against her. The cancer, like an unwelcome guest, has made itself at home and has no plans to ever leave. Unfortunately, this time, both of you, my dear sweet sons, will remember this struggle and will, I hope, learn from it.

As I watch her, fighting for her life, I commit to walking this path with her for however long it will take. Even though I am afraid and sad, I do have hope (borne in a spirit of faith and trust) that she will survive this battle. I am praying that she will win and that the cancer, at least on this terrain and in this body, will concede, throw up a white flag, and retreat.

the cancer journals: an ending

May 4, 2013

...from my diary

February 20, 2013: Dear Mother Flo: this week has been revelatory and has forced me to grow up. The first is that your grandson has become a tweenager. He went to bed on Saturday as a wrinkled ashy faced nappy headed little boy who was afraid of monsters and things that go bump in the night and woke up looking for lotion, trying to iron his clothes, using every hair product we have in the house, and talking about girls. Second, I spoke at the White House this week. My dream has always been to speak to the world about the importance of black history—my passion. I never could have imagined that I would be selected, out of all of the scholars in the country, to be one of four to speak on this panel. I felt like I walked on water and that no door would ever be closed to me. I felt fearless and courageous, a scholar with a cape and a "S" on my chest. And finally, you got diagnosed with Stage IV lung cancer and my world, at that moment, became very small.

March 25, 2013: You fell today and I was not strong enough to help you. I felt helpless, like a spectator at an event. I could not participate though I suffered with you. I bear witness to your pain and I wonder where you learned to stand it. You are from rural North Carolina, a bastion of racism and poverty, perhaps learning how to be strong in the face of incredible odds was something you learned as a child. I stood outside your room for just a moment, as I had to catch my breath and steel myself for what lay before me. I did not know exactly what to expect, as so much had happened so quickly. I told myself to smile even if I wanted to cry. The last thing I wanted to do was mix my tears of fear with yours. You should not have to shoulder my pain along with your own.

April 7, 2013: I woke up today thinking that you were going to beat this thing called cancer. You were going to be a survivor and we were going to look back on this thing called cancer and laugh, recognizing that we as black women and black people had survived the Middle Passage, American enslavement and apartheid, WWI and II, Vietnam and Reagonomics so surely we could survive this thing called cancer.

April 12, 2013: I wish I could give you my strength, my optimism, and my "live in the moment" pure joy. I want to remind you of who you used to be and how vivacious you used to be. I just want to tell you over and over again that I see you and I remember what your life was like before cancer showed up.

April 24, 2013: I do not know how to say goodbye. My grandmother, when my grandfather passed away after a two-year battle with prostate cancer, told me that she simply said, "Until that morning." She said that there will a come a morning, when the trumpet will sound and the dead in Christ will rise first and those of us who are still here will be caught up to meet Him in the sky. On that morning, she will see my grandfather again. She said that when they were younger and newly married, instead of saying goodbye they would say "Until this evening," or "Until tomorrow." Goodbyes are final and when you love someone there is no goodbye it is only an until.

REFLECTIONS

I hate losing. I hate it when I lose my keys, lose my way, or lose my train of thought. I was raised in a very competitive household and I learned early on from my father that we never give up and that we always fight until the end. I always followed my father's advice and I have very rarely lost. He used to tell me that when I fall, and I will fall, I should fall on my back because if I look up, I can get it. I know how to lose, I just hate doing it. I have spent my life trying to learn the rules of every game that I played in an effort to ensure that I was always prepared and that I had everything that I needed to be victorious. I believed that things always balanced out and that if you knew the rules and you fought hard then you would never lose. The game always made sense to me when I knew the rules. I respected the boundaries and I fought hard. I am not accustomed to or comfortable with losing and that is why I am having a difficult time.

On April 24, less than three months after being diagnosed with Stage IV lung cancer that had metastasized from her lungs to two places in her brain, my dear sweet mother-in-law, your grandmother, passed away. I used to tell people that she was fighting lung cancer but in reality, she was not. Although she had completed six weeks of radiation to her brain and she was taking an oral chemotherapy drug, she was getting noticeably weaker everyday. She went from being a robust and vibrant person to being on complete bed rest in less than a month. She stopped talking to me and though she would look at me when I came into the room, she did not acknowledge me. I wonder if there was a part of her proud spirit that was angry that someone other than her children had to witness her pain. I remember the last time she walked. It was on March 25, about six weeks after she had been diagnosed. and she went to the doctor's office to get an update on her condition. When we got back to the house, your father, and two of his siblings were trying to help her get up the stairs and into the house. When she fell for the second time, I jumped out of the car to try and be of some assistance. Your grandmother was a heavy woman, about 5'9 maybe 285 pounds, and there were four of us trying to help her. Even though your daddy was behind her, your uncle was in front of her, your aunt was on the right side and I was on the left, when she fell to the ground again, we all went down with her. It took everything we had to get her up the stairs and into the house. I felt helpless. The doctor said that because of the radiation to her brain, her body was acting like she had had a stroke so the left side of her body had just stopped working. In so many ways, so did we.

When someone you love gets diagnosed with a terminal disease, your life, as you know it, stops working. You lose touch and you lose track of time. The days slip by and though you are going to work or to school, you are not fully present anywhere. It is as if the universe demands everything you have to give and makes you focus all of your attention and energy on trying to keep your loved one alive. I could feel myself almost trying to will her back to good health. Cancer became real to me again and this time, it was everywhere. I would hold conversations with cancer and demand that it answer my questions about what I could do to force it to leave your grandmother alone. I got angry at cancer. I fussed at it, ignored it, and apologized to it. In my mind, cancer was like a spider that had caught my mother-in-law in a web and everyone who was connected to her was caught as well. There were days when I convinced myself that we were winning and days when I knew that we were not. Her cancer was aggressive and mean and relentless. It was smart and was always about two steps in front of us. It was playing a game that had no rules. When we attempted to fight the cancer in the lungs, it moved to the brain and when we went after the cancer in the brain, it moved to the lower gastrointestinal tract. I remember the day we found out that it had moved from the lower gastrointestinal tract to the trachea, this was the day when I realized that we were fighting a battle that we would not win. By that time, she had not walked in a month, had not smiled or laughed or spoken to me in two months, and I had not exhaled in close to three.

I was walking around in a semi-comatose state just waiting for the next thing, to hear the next place where cancer had taken up residence or the next remedy that the doctors wanted to try. I was a weary traveler. I remember when I was 22 and I was hiking with a group trying to get to the top of Mt. Kilimanjaro. When we were about halfway up the mountain, one of my traveling companions—a very nice young white girl from the Midwest who was traveling with her black boyfriend and who constantly complained about how her parents did not accept her radical lifestyle—came down with altitude sickness and she needed to go back down the mountain. We met as a group and decided that since we had come this far together, we would all go back down with her. At the time, I thought I would be back because in my mind, Tanzania was a place where I would spend some significant portions of my life. It has been over twenty years and I have never been back. I regret not going forward and instead choosing to go back down with people I had just met and have never seen again. I took my eyes off my own personal goals. I should have gone forward. I felt the same way when I looked at your grandmother laying in bed, unable to move or to speak and in incredible pain even after radiation, physical therapy, and oral chemotherapy. I felt that we had been so focused on trying to beat cancer that we had taken our eyes off our goal, which should have been to enjoy the time we had left with our mother. We should have just made her comfortable.

I am not an expert on cancer or on dying but I do know, after bearing witness to her struggle for the past three months, that lung cancer is a horrible horrible way to die. She was in constant pain. She could not move, speak, laugh, or interact in any significant way. She could not feed herself or go to the bathroom or use the remote to change the channels. I used to look her and pray that the Lord would either heal her or take her home. How hard it must have been for her to be trapped inside her own body. I hope that she knew that we were doing everything we could and that if love alone was enough to heal her, she would have been healed.

We buried her in North Carolina, right next to her mother. At the funeral, my job was to pay tribute to her. She once laughed and told me that she wanted me to write a poem and read it at her funeral. I thought about her life, her spirit, and how much she loved me when I got up and spoke. I remember that the two of you were crying and you had your heads down. I told you to look up because we were celebrating a life, well lived. She was a fore-runner, a trailblazer. She was a woman who knew her own mind and was not easily swayed by others. She stood tall and firm for the truth, as she interpreted it to be. I talked about the meaning of her life and what we were suppose to receive from her passing into the quiet recesses of our mind and how we had to go forward even if we did not want to do so. I said that we should learn from her mistakes and grow from her lessons. We must be the ones to remember her and to not forget that she was human and that she got it right more often than she got it wrong. I said that she confirmed life and she confirmed us. And then, right before I sat down, I looked over at the two of you and then at your father and then down at her casket, and I simply said, "Until that morning."

reds could have been harriet

August 16, 2013

I. On Russell Simmons, Moses, and the Push for Freedom

As you know, it takes a lot for me to be surprised by what people say and do, as I usually expect the best from people and am disappointed (but not surprised) when I do not receive it. I pride myself on being a fair person who gives people the benefit of the doubt. I try to see people for who they are and I do my best to accept them despite their obvious faults and flaws. At the same time, in this age of technology and reality television, I know that people will do and say just about anything for money and fame. Even though I do not agree with the way the world is moving, I do accept that it is moving and that I need to make decisions about how much I want to move with it. I am a realist and somewhat of a pragmatist having grown up between Washington, DC, where I was surrounded by forward thinking black people, and South Carolina, where I visited stores that still had their "For Colored Only" signs taped to the wall. As someone who studies black women's history and who has read the Holy Bible more than once, I feel that I have read so much material (on topics that range from rape to slavery, incest and war, physical abuse and domestic violence) that my heart is almost hardened to the realities of this world. And yet, I found myself surprised, shocked, and hurt when you told me that your class had a lunchtime discussion about the Harriet Tubman sex tape.

I thought you were mistaken because no one associates the memory of Tubman with sex but when I pulled up Russell Simmons' "webisode," I realized that I was watching a shift in her image and in the ways that her life and her work will be discussed and remembered. As I sat there, watching this distasteful clip, tears were rolling down my face as the young actress portraying Tubman began to seduce her plantation owner and joke about how she much she enjoyed their secret times together. I was (and still am) angry with Russell Simmons and people like him who are willing to do anything for money. I felt sorry for the actress and the other actors who agreed to be a part of this project and I believe that they also should be ashamed, shamed, and embarrassed. I realize that in this age of technology, no matter how much you sacrifice to make the world better you could still end up as a star in someone else's sex tape. I have never been a Russell Simmons fan but after watching the video, I spent countless hours trying to find out more about him as I needed to understand what would compel a sane person to support, fund, and promote this type of work. I realized that Simmons, like most people in America, either does not know his history or does not value it—because at some point, your life should be about more than wanting to make money (though he seems to do that very well), it should be about making the decision in your spirit that there are some things that you will never do just to make money.

He is not the first person to cross that line and create a permanent record that moves our people and the struggle in the opposite direction and sadly, we know that he will not be the last. I take comfort in the fact that even though people will continue to cross that line, there is a community of people who will actively speak out against it. They will push back and though we will never get back to where we use to be (because this video of Harriet Tubman was published online, it is now a part of our permanent records), we can make people aware of where we stand on these issues in an effort to avoid it from happening again. Harriet Tubman is a legend. She is a shero. She is one of our maternal mothers. And therefore, she should be untouchable.

II. Harriet Tubman, My Childhood Myths and Legend

I remember the first time I pretended to be Harriet Tubman. I was eight years old and I was on my way to water to think. I use to spend every summer at Reds' farm in Lexington, South Carolina. She used to go fishing every day in her lake that sat at the end of the woods on her property. She probably had somewhere between 7-10 acres of land, most of it was woods. She had a path through the trees where she used to make us walk down to the water and sit whenever we got in trouble. It always felt like we walking our last mile. She would stand at the entrance to the woods and would watch us as we walked down to the lake. I remember this because I used to get in trouble quite a bit as a young girl. She would tell me to go and sit by the water and think about everything I had done so that I could figure out a way to "be better." She would say, "I'm gonna watch you all the way to the water and just because you can't see me doesn't mean that I won't see you."

I use to walk through the woods pretending to be Harriet Tubman leading my people to freedom. I would pick up a stick and put it in my waistband and pull it out like a gun when the runaway slaves would talk about going back to Egypt. I would duck down in the trees and tell everybody to quiet down so I could hear the dogs and come up with a plan to hide from them. I used to look up and pretend to see the North Star or touch the sides of the trees feeling around for moss. When I got down to the lake, I would pretend that we were in the Promised Land and I would get down on my knees and kiss the ground. I would shout, "You all are free now, ain't nobody gon make you do anything that you don't wanna do, no mo'." I would do a little dance and sing, "I looked at my hands and my hands looked new and I looked at my feet and my feet did too." I would sit by the water and think about Harriet Tubman, the Moses of my people. A black woman who put her body on the line over and over again to lead people to freedom. I always thought that she was more courageous than Moses of the Holy Bible, particularly since he told God more than once that he did not want to go and she went willingly over and over again. I admired her for her courage and loved her for her fierce feminist spirit.

Reds could have easily been a Moses. She taught me how to fish, shoot pigs, garden, climb trees, fight my male cousins, and paint. She would tell me that Anderson women never lose because they were born fighters and winners. When she took me fishing, she used to make me walk to the lake with my eyes closed so that I would know how to get there and get back to the house on my own. She said that the only thing worse then being lost on your land was not knowing who you were and what you were capable of doing. She was probably the first person who ever talked about Harriet as if she was a woman and not just a mythical being.

When I learned about Harriet in school, my teachers never talked about her as a woman or as a wife. They never mentioned her childhood and what it must have been like growing up on a plantation as a young girl. They did not spend much time talking about her life with her first husband, a free man who coupled with an enslaved woman and chose to live with her on a plantation or her second husband, a young veteran she married after the Civil

War. I never thought about how much courage it took for her, as a young woman, to make the decision to leave her family, her friends, and her husband in search of this thing called freedom. Harriet Tubman ran away by herself to a place that she had only heard about but had never seen. I never understood that she was disabled. I knew that she had been hit in the head by a piece of iron but it never dawned on me until my Reds pointed out that Harriet was a woman who probably suffered from intense headaches and would often fall asleep at a moment's notice. And yet, despite all of the odds facing her, she chose to run towards something that, in her mind, had to better than what she had. She embodied courage and hope and freedom. She had grit, that elusive hard to define quality that separates women like Harriet Tubman and Rosa Parks and Fannie Lou Hamer and Shirley Chisholm and grandma Reds from the rest of us.

I have always wanted to be Harriet Tubman. I wanted to be the type of person that would always choose to go back and help other people to be free. I did not want to be Frederick Douglass because he only saved himself and I did not want to be Henry Box Brown because he only mailed himself. I did not want to be Ellen and William Craft because they only saved themselves. I did not even want to be Moses from the Old Testament because he made only one trip and he did it reluctantly. I wanted to be Harriet, a modern-day Moses leading my people to the Promised Land over and over again. I wanted my name to be whispered and remembered like hers. I wanted to be immortal because when your name and your story are remembered then you are never really gone. I used to walk through the woods on the way to the water singing "Steal Away" or "Go Down Moses" or "Wade in the Water" at the top of my lungs. I was Moses and I was on my way to freedom and I was not looking back.

III. Going Down as Moses to Tell Old Russell to Let My Sister Go!

I thought about all of that when I watched Russell Simmons's Harriet Tubman video. I thought about it when I got sick to my stomach, when I deleted it, and when I took a shower because I felt dirty after watching it. I do not know Russell Simmons but I do know that anyone who would produce this work and laugh about it is someone who is enslaved and needs to be saved (even if it is only from themselves). Harriet Tubman could have freed a lot more people if they had known they were enslaved and my job today is to make sure that those who are enslaved are told about it and given a chance to be free. When you first visited Loyola University Maryland, one of my colleagues told you that his favorite quote was that "the world is charged with the grandeur of God," you responded that it was now our job to" safe keep" the grandeur. You had the right idea then and that is the same work that you and your brother must do to "safe keep", guard, and protect our history.

discovering auntie maya[3]

May 28, 2014

When you got into the car today, I told you that my heart had stopped earlier in the day, for just a moment. The same way it stopped when I heard that Toni Cade Bambara had colon cancer and when I heard that Nelson Mandela had passed away. It stopped the same way that my grandmother's heart stopped when she received the news about the assassinations of John F. Kennedy, Jr., Martin Luther King Jr., Medgar Evers, and the Four Little Girls.[4] It stopped the same way that your heart stopped when we lost your grandmother, Florence Huzzey, and your cousin, Carson Eugene III. It was only for a moment but I realized that with the loss of Maya Angelou, the world had lost a giant and for some of us, things would never be the same again. It was hard for me, at that moment, to imagine living in a world without the voice and the energy of Dr. Angelou. She had, in the words of my grandmother, "run on ahead to see how the end was going to be and how her story was going to start again." My grandmother would say that death was just the ending of this journey and the beginning of the next experience

I. On the Pulse of the Morning

I have always thought of Maya Angelou as the spiritual consciousness of our nation, embodying the best of who we are and everything that we should strive to become. I remember in 1993 when she spoke at President Clinton's inauguration—becoming only the second poet and the first Black woman to read a poem at a presidential inauguration—and she invited everyone in her poem "...the Asian, the Hispanic, the Jew/ The African and Native American, the Sioux/ The Catholic, the Muslim, the French, the Greek/ The Irish, the Rabbi, the Priest, the Sheikh/ The Gay, the Straight, the Preacher/ The privileged, the homeless, the Teacher" to come and plant themselves beside the river because their descendants had paved and paid the way for them to be there. I cried then as she laid out her vision for a new America, a place where all voices would be included and respected, a place where we could truly "give birth again to the dream" and lift up our eyes for the new day breaking for us. When she said that she was "the Tree planted by the River, Which will not be moved" she was talking about and for us all. America has this history, that has been shaped and nurtured by very painful (and sometimes shameful) events but if we face out past with courage then we do not—as Angelou reminded us—either have to relive them or apologize for them. We have this history and with those lessons in mind we can take the future in the "palms of our hands" and "Mold it into the shape of (our) most Private need." And then, we can "Sculpt it into The image of (our) most public self."[5] This is how she lived her life, molding and shaping her past private needs into her powerful public self.

She was a force that had been shaped and nurtured by a difficult childhood, one in which she chose to remain silent for almost five years. She was a survivor and when she finally spoke to the world through her writing, her music, and her art, she spoke volumes. She made me feel brave, and on days when I felt like I could not go on, her poetry and her stories would make me stand a little bit higher and push me to go a little bit farther.

II. And Still I Rise

I received my copy of "I Know Why the Caged Bird Sings" when I was 16 years old, full of angst and crying over yet another boyfriend lost.[6] My mother walked into my room, laid the book on my bed, and said, "Read it. It will make you strong. It will give you light, and it will teach you how to sing." I did and it did. It was one of the books (along with Alice Walker's *The Temple of My Familiar* and Angelou's fifth autobiography, *All God's Children Need Traveling Shoes*) that I carried with me to Ghana in hopes of retracing Maya Angelou's steps. It was the first of her seven autobiographies and I have read and devoured nearly all of them, highlighting passages, making comments in the margins as I tested and tasted each word and then made them my own.

I remember watching the movie "Roots" in 1977 and when Maya Angelou appeared on screen, your grandfather started clapping and stood up. He then told us that when genius appears in your midst, you must stand up and mark the moment. My father, who grew up in South Carolina and was involved in the civil rights movement, does not know her as Maya Angelou the poet; he remembers her as a freedom fighter, as the person who walked with Martin and met with Malcolm. He remembers watching her dance and hearing her sing. He remembers when she performed and the world seemed to come alive around her. He remembers her as a spiritual sister; I tend to remember her as a spiritual aunt — a regal woman who gave advice and guidance.

III. Connections

I met her twice, and although I did not know her well, I claimed her words, her experiences, and her life as a part of my own. I used to teach her poem, "And Still I Rise," to women at the correctional center and at a women's shelter reminding them over and over again that the power to rise comes from within and that where you story starts (where you come from) does not have to be where your story ends.[7] Your story –like Maya Angelou's story—can be shaped by you. You can name yourself and find a space that belongs to you. This is what she taught me, how to celebrate life and interpret and define the beauty that is inside of you.

I met her for the first time in 1999—shortly after I won The Langston Hughes, David Diop, Etheridge Knight Poetry Award from the Gwendolyn Brooks Creative Writing Center—at an awards ceremony in which my writing was being honored. She was walking through the crowd and when she was introduced to me, she grabbed my hands and said, "Keep writing baby, the world needs your words." I met her again in 2002 under similar circumstances. I was pregnant for the second time, and I was complaining about being exhausted all of the time. I asked her to give me some advice on how to keep moving forward when everything in you wants to stop going. She took my copy of her first autobiography — the one that I was clutching in my hand, the one that my mother had given me when I was 16 — and wrote the word "joy" in capital letters. She then said, "Do everything with joy… !" Although it has been fifteen years since she told me to keep writing and twelve since she told me to do everything with joy, I remember both of these moments as if they have just happened. These were extraordinary moments, the ones that I will never forget, the ones that continue to challenge me. I never had a chance to thank her for showing us what it means to be fully present in a moment, for writing her life stories for all the world to see, and for living every moment with joy.

IV. Until…

Today just for a moment, my heart stopped and then as I remembered Maya Angelou and everything that she has given the world, and me, I smiled and gave thanks for her life, well lived.

the bridge across forever

July 28, 2012

When you were four years old, I read you a book about a seagull that wanted to be more than what they told him he was destined to become. You spent the day running around the back yard pretending that you could fly and rolling around on the grass pretending to do double rolls. You thought it was funny that a seagull could talk. When you turned eight, we read Richard Bach's book about a reluctant Messiah and we tried to imagine why someone would choose to give up the gifts that they have been given. We talked about the importance of gifts and how they were not given to us but entrusted in us to be used to make the world better. When you turned ten, we read Bach's book about a bridge that possibly extended forever. We then thought about what we do if we were able to send a letter back in time to the person we used to be? You wanted to know which "me" would I choose to communicate with and what would I say? And even more important, how would I know that my letter had arrived and that the "me" that I contacted had taken my advice?

I thought about the *Back to the Future* movies where one change in the fabric of history, changed everything in his future but him. What started as a simple question really had me thinking long and hard about my life, the choices I have made, and the impact of those decisions. At 40+ years old, I now have the benefit of seeing the long-arm of history and how so many small decisions made in haste with very little thought have become the pillars of the life that I have constructed for myself.

I have never been a reflective decision maker; instead, I tended to pray, make a decision very quickly, and just hope for the best. I believe that things do have a way of working out for the best and I have learned to trust myself enough to make a decision and stand by it. I have had so many adventures in my life from backpacking through East Africa to living with a blind woman on a mountain in Chemundu; from seeing the black Madonna to literally watching the moon "rise" on a fishing boat off the coast of Lamu; I tried unsuccessfully to climb Mount Kilimanjaro but made it to the top of the hot springs mountain in Wondo Genet; I have been roller skating in South Africa and bicycling in Paris; I cried when I stepped through the "Door of No Return" in Senegal and when I was learning how to breathe "Benedictine" style in Minnesota; I have lived in a Peace House in Indiana and in a tent in Shashamane; I became an adopted member of a tribe in Tanzania and I pledged a sorority at Lincoln University; and, I met my soul/mate when I moved to New York without a job to live and work as an independent filmmaker. I have stumbled onto more jobs, adventures, opportunities, and really good people simply because one thread of an experience has typically led me to another one.

What would I tell myself if I could get a letter back in time? When I first thought about it I decided to send a letter to the 16-year old girl that I used to be. I remember that that was the last year before I started to really believe that I knew everything. When I turned 17, something clicked in my brain. I felt like I had become an expert on the world and that there were very few people who could tell me anything. It took me years to break through this and to realize and recognize how little I knew about the world and about myself. My Nana used to tell me that if I ever forgot who I was I should call her because she would remind me. I have called her and asked her this question more times than I care to remember. (I thought I would tell my 16-year old self to go and find your father so that they can marry early and not have to suffer so many heartaches before they found one another. When I shared this with him, he pointed out that when I was 16, he was 21 and he would not have listened to or spent time with me.)

I thought about the bad decisions that I had made and how I could use my letter to warn her about them. I then realized that every past "bad" decision helped me to make better future decisions. My scars, just like my grey hair and my wrinkles, are a part of who I am. It has taken me years to accept this about myself and to understand that those decisions are the building blocks that are holding me up and helping me to move forward. Those decisions made me who I am and they are helping me to shape you into who you will eventually become. I am trying so hard to do for you what your grandparents did for me —to be your "Catcher in the Rye," using my experiences to shield you, to mold you, to shape you, and to ultimately let you go. My parents pushed me out of the nest and then flew in front of me when I followed, behind me when I strayed, and beside me when I faltered. My parents taught me well.

With all of these thoughts in mind, my letter to my 16-year old self would actually be very short – I would thank her for being who she was, tell her that I loved her, and tell her that despite what she may think or how she may be feeling at that moment, everything will (and does) work out. This is how I want you to live your life, with no apologies and no regrets. I want you to embrace and experience and enjoy every moment and realize that every failure and every success are only small parts of your adventure. You have a long way to go and the only way to get there is to keep moving forward.

Nurturing Masculinity

a forerunner's journey

teaching you how to fly

January 11, 2014

Kofi:

Thirteen years ago when I first saw you and I looked in your beautiful brown face and your clear eyes, my heart just leaped. I felt as if everything good and pure and real about your father and I had been poured into you. Today you are a teenager, a young man. I did not know, when I woke up this morning, how hard today was going to be for me. I had heard about this day and I thought that I was ready, I was not. When you got up and I walked in to the kitchen, you wanted to know why I started crying. I realized, at that moment, that my baby boy—the one I had given birth to and held in my arms; loved and disciplined; the one who knows how to make me laugh and has (more often than you know) made me cry in frustration; one of the reasons why I do the work that I do—had become a young man. My dear sweet boy, thank you for your childhood and I am now ready to mother the man that you are becoming. You have incredible shoes to fill and like the men whose name that you carry, you have the potential to be more than what you are and what others will ever expect for you to become.

As we stand here at the intersection between the child that you used to be and the man you are becoming, I wanted to take a moment to remind you of the best of who you are. We live in a time where black men are once again under attack, where they are expected to underachieve, and underperform. This is a time when young black boys are not safe and are not being nurtured and cared for or given the skills they need to navigate and negotiate through these very difficult environments. I have spent the last thirteen years watching you and I have done all that I can to plant good seeds in your soil. I have tried to be a eagle that has guided you along the way.

I. Become An Eagle

Granddaddy once told me a story about a little boy who found an eagle's egg on the ground. Since he could not put the egg back where it belonged, he decided to place the eagle's egg into a chicken's nest. When the eagle was born, he was taught over and over again how to peck upon the ground for corn. He used to tell his brothers how he wanted to fly and how he wanted to soar; but, they would remind him that he was a chicken and chickens don't soar, they peck. They told him to forget his dream and focus on what was in front of him. Although he pecked everyday, he was never able to still that quiet voice that kept telling him that he could fly. One day as he pecked along a female eagle, bold and beautiful, approached him and asked him who he was and why he was here. He answered, "I'm a chicken and I peck."

The eagle asked him, "Do you want to fly?" And he said, "I can't, I'm a chicken." She said, "But don't you want to soar?" And he said, "No, I can't I'm a chicken." She then said as she began to turn around if you want to catch the wind and experience life beyond what your eye can see, follow me. And though everything in him told him not to go, he went anyway because he still had that secret desire to fly. The eagle led him up to the top of the mountain and as he looked out over the edge, she pushed him off and then jumped off as well She yelled to him as he begin to fall, "Flap your winds and trust the process." As he started to do this she flew right underneath him and said, "If you fall, I will catch you." As he began to straighten up, the eagle came and flew beside him, "You're flying now," she said, "but if you want to soar, you have got to trust the process and stop flapping your wings." She flew in front of him and showed him how to flap less and soar more. As he began to soar, she came down beside him and asked him was he ready to catch the wind. She told him that he needed to pull in front of her and lead the way. Even though he was scared, he realized that he was already flying and soaring so he decided to fly out in front of her.

She flew behind him until she was sure that he was steady and solid and then she came up beside him one last time. "Do you know who I am?" He shook his head and she said, "I'm an eagle and I'm your mother and that means that you are also an eagle. You were not meant to peck on the ground for corn. You were born to fly and to soar. Your history does not determine your destiny although your history is a part of your destiny. Remember, my dear sweet son, who you are." She then fell behind him and allowed him to go off and find his way.

Kofi, I have been your older eagle and though the world has told you more than once that you are only here to peck on the ground I want to remind you that you were meant to fly and to soar. I have flown beneath you and in front of you but now as you become a teenager, my role is to fly beside you as you begin to figure out your way, and behind you as you begin to fly off in pursuit of your own path.

II. Your *Examen*

As you begin the next leg of your journey, I want you to think deeply about these three Jesuit questions that might help you to figure out your way. I have spent the last couple of years asking you these questions and at thirteen, it is time for you to ask yourself:

What brings you joy? Some people confuse joy with happiness, but they are not the same. Happiness is fleeting and is based on your feelings and dependent upon things happening. Joy on the other hand is deep rooted and even though your circumstance may not be perfect, you still feel good when you are engaged in this activity. Joy, Kofi, is something that the world does not give it nor can it take it away from you. Remember this when people try to define for you what brings you joy. You have to own it, claim it, and you need to guard it. You are the only one who can decide what brings you joy. You have to think deeply about all those things that you enjoy doing and begin to decide which of the things bring you happiness and which of them bring you joy.

What are you good at? This is a really difficult question to answer and there are some who spend their life trying to find the answer. The first question is one that you can answer on your own but for this one, you will need a little help. I say this because some of the things that really bring you joy may not be the things that you are good at doing. When I was younger, singing bought me so much joy. I used to sing in front of the mirror and imagine myself in front of a large crowd of people. I remember when I told granddaddy that I wanted to quit school and join a band. He was so supportive and he went out bought me a tape recorder. He asked me to record my favorite song and then bring it to him so we could listen to it together. I sat there crying as I heard this voice, my voice, doing everything but sing on key. It was heart wrenching. At the end, as I sat there with tears rolling down my face, my father asked me if I still wanted to join a band I shook my head and stood up very quietly and very slowly. My father put his arms around me and pulled my face up to look at him. He then told me that just because I had a love for something does not mean it is what God has sent me to here to do. He told me not to worry because there will come a time when the thing that I love and the thing that I can do line up with one another, He said that when that happens I will have a head on collision with my purpose and I will be actively doing the work that God has sent me here to do. Sometimes other people—people who love you—can help you to get the answer to this question and then if it brings you job, then you are almost where you need to be.

Where does God need you to do this in the world? Once you figure out what brings you joy and where your talents lay then you need to figure out where you need to be. You have to believe that God has you here for a reason and there is a place where He needs you to be to do this work. You also must understand that your vocation may change because "vocation," someone once said, "always leads to vocation." You discover your vocation when the things that bring you joy connect with the things that you are good at doing and they meet the need that the world has at that moment. All of my life I have always said that I wanted to be a lawyer. I had dreams of being the next Thurgood Marshall or Barbara Jordan. At the end of my junior year, I decided that I wanted to move to Africa to find myself and figure out what I really wanted to do. I moved to Nairobi and spent months traveling, meeting people, and asking myself some very tough questions. I was in search of myself and this search has taken me farther than I ever thought I would go. I came back to America and decided to go to graduate school instead of law school. I also decided to do in America exactly what I did in Africa: to go wherever the wind takes me, trust the process, let the answers and the path come to me. I remember that every time I called granddaddy and told him that I was quitting something in search of the next adventure, he would always say, "I can not tell you what to do or where to go but I can remind you that you know the way and I know that you know it because I taught it to you." I went from working with the

Writer's Corps to graduate school in Indiana; to working in New York as a documentary filmmaker and a television producer to getting married and having two boys. We moved from New York to Baltimore and I became a middle school teacher for four years before I quit and became a full-time doctoral student. I finished my program with distinction and now I am a professor at Loyola and the mother of two young men. Along the way, I have made so many mistakes and I have fallen over and over again. There have been so many times when it was difficult for me to move forward but I had to move forward despite how I was feeling. Although I did not always know where to go or how to get there, I did know that I knew the way.

Kofi, if you trust yourself, trust the training that we have given you, and trust that still quiet voice that God has placed inside of you, you will indeed realize that you know the way. My job is no longer to tell you where to go, it is simply to remind you that you know the way. I look forward to being there on that day when you discover what gives you joy, what you are good at doing, and where God wants you to do this in the world.

commit yourself to being ordinary

October 15, 2014

I woke up this morning and realized that in just two years, I will celebrate my 25th college reunion. I remember the day when I graduated because that was the moment when I felt invincible. I felt that the world was mine and that I could bend it and shape it to meet my will. I felt brilliant as if I was going to change the world, cure cancer, and end world poverty. I felt like I was special and that I was the one that the world had been waiting for to solve the hard problems. I had been told that I was smart and I had been given multiple opportunities to prove it. It has been almost twenty-five years and I realized this morning that I have yet to change the world. I also realized, in that same moment, that I am no longer interested in trying to do so.

I actually do not believe that is possible to change the entire world; instead, I now believe that the best that we can do is try to change ourselves and focus on making the people and the situations around us a little bit better. This morning I watched David McCullough Jr.'s 2012 Commencement Speech to the graduating class of Wellesley High School where he told them, over and over again, that they were not special. This only confirmed what I already knew, despite what I was told twenty-five years ago, I am not special either; in fact, I am pretty ordinary.[8] As I have gotten older and I have watched my parents' age and I have tried to teach you to make the right choices, I have come to understand that this experiment that we call life is special but the everyday living is not. Life is hard and it is full of challenges and disappointments, extraordinary moments and ordinary days. It is full of paying bills, going to work, and working hard to find meaning in your own reality. It is about standing up for what you believe in and walking away from situations that are damaging to your spirit. It is about learning how to see beyond your own life so that you can help those who have a greater more pressing need at that moment. The hardest part of life is realizing that even if you do not actively participate in making it better, it is going to continue; and, like we have seen in the lives of people like Martin Luther King, Jr., Medgar Evers, John F. Kennedy, and Patrice Lumumba, life is going to continue even without you.

You cannot control the fact that you are growing older but you can and do control growing up. You, alone, have to make this decision and it is a necessary and important rite of passage. You must realize, though this realization will hurt and sober you, that despite what I have led you to believe, you are not special. In the same way that McCullough challenged the graduating class, I challenge you, my dear sweet sons, to think about what it means to be ordinary because ordinary people are the ones who push us to be better than what we are. I challenge you to actively reject being defined as special and instead—be you, be ordinary, and be an active participant in this experiment. Do the simple things like pay your taxes, look both ways before you cross the street, and speak up when you see someone being bullied. Be ordinary and volunteer at the local shelter, help kids learn how to read, and root for the underdog.

You, more than any other generation, have been coddled and

loved, you have been protected and pampered, you have been caught before you have fallen and shown how to fly before you were taught how to crawl. You have learned, through social media, how to document every aspect of your life and how to be a star in your own eyes. I blame myself (and my generation) for this as we have done this to you. We told you that you were special and then we put every piece of technology in your hands and helped you to project your "specialness" onto the world. We have not allowed you to fail or to even make decisions on your own. We have micromanaged every part of your life so that we could feel special through you. I challenge you to adopt the same spirit that Martin Luther had when he wrote and posted his Ninety-Five Theses or that Ida Bell Wells-Barnett had when she was forcibly removed from a train and sued the railroad company, and consciously reject this label and instead seek to be ordinary. Find moments when you can be introspective and write about it in a journal instead of posting it up on Facebook. Lose yourself in a moment and resist the urge to take a picture of the moment to share with the world. Be ordinary, try something new and if you fail at it, laugh and start something else.

Being ordinary is similar to having grit, which means that you are committed to getting back up every time you fall, you work hard to learn from both your successes and your failures, you are not consumed with your own life, and you are an active participant in making your little piece of forever better. Special people want to but can never change the world; ordinary people are the ones who keep the world moving forward and hopefully, moving forward in the right direction. I look forward to being there on that day when you embrace what it means to be ordinary and when you embrace the work that you were meant to do.

the road to peace does not begin with war![9]

September 7, 2013

When you were growing up, you were very selfish, and you demanded a lot of attention. You learned the word "mine" and then proceeded to use it to describe everything that you could see. You used to push and hit and stomp you feet over and over again while I patiently taught you how to share and not to hit. I taught you that violence was never an answer and that the best way to solve a problem was to talk about it and find a way to compromise.

I used incidents that happened on the playground and in the classroom as teachable moments to talk to you about the path of nonviolence. I made sure that you were familiar with the teachings of Jesus Christ, Mahatma Gandhi, Thich Nhat Hanh, James Farmer, and Martin Luther King, Jr. and that you understood that nonviolence was not passive resistance. It is an act of courage to stand tall in the face of violence and conflict, whether it is happening on the playgrounds of Baltimore or in the hallways of Congress.

This path of practicing nonviolence has not always been easy for either one of you. You have been bullied and teased and have had to learn how to walk away. You have learned how to pray for your enemies and how to meet hate and intolerance with love and patience. I tried to remind you (almost as much as I remind myself) that the universe, as Dr. King once said, is on the side of justice and that these moments of controversy and confusion are the ones that shape their character. There was a time, early on, when I foolishly believed that all parents were teaching their children the same thing: how to choose love instead of hate, nonviolence instead of violence, and how to listen to one another and seek compromise instead of accepting chaos and confusion. I believed that we were working together to be the type of change that we wanted to see in the world.

One of the reasons that I voted for Barack Obama was that I was convinced that he was a man who believed in and fought for peace. He campaigned on a platform of change, and I thought that meant a change from all of the policies that have led us into Afghanistan and Vietnam and have led us to bomb Iraq, Somalia, Pakistan, Yemen and, in one sad case in 1985, a neighborhood in West Philadelphia. I was excited when he was awarded the Nobel Peace Prize, confident that anyone who is bestowed such an honor must be a passionate believer in and a crusader for peace. I think of other Nobel Peace Prize winners, like Mother Theresa, Wangari Muta Maathai, Liu Xiaobo, Tawakkol Karmane, and Malala Yousafzai, to name just a few, whose very lives have been spent working to create a more peaceful, just and verdant world.

This is why I was so horrified when I sat with you and we listened while President Obama talked about bombing Syria with the same type of casualness that one talks about shopping. He mentioned that there would not be any "boots on the ground," as if hundreds (or maybe thousands) of innocent men, women, and children will not be impacted when bombs drop from planes that are being driven by men and women who are miles away from the center of death and destruction. He talked as if the only way to establish peace was to attack first and then negotiate with anyone who was still standing at the end. I almost laughed when I remembered his "red line," because as both a parent and an activist, I always knew that it would come back to haunt him and would force him to make this type of decision.

I could not understand nor could I explain to you why we were seeking to establish peace in the world without first establishing it at home. I do understand that there are some valid reasons why Mr. Obama and others feel that we must move forward and that we are once again called upon to be the peacekeepers for the entire world. I thought long and hard about this as I sat and wrote a letter to our president:

> Dear sir: now that you have drawn a line in the sand and have decided that America is once again called upon to be the peacekeepers for the entire world, I offer you the cities of Baltimore, Chicago, Atlanta, and New York (to name just a few) as places that would benefit from your love and attention. If peace is really the goal then we should start by promoting peace at home—in the cities across America where people are dying and starving; where they are unemployed and underemployed; where our kids are dropping out of schools or spending countless hours playing senseless violent video games and listening to violent misogynistic rap lyrics; where folks live in sub standard housing within food deserts; where murder, violence, rape, drugs, crime, and gang activity are accepted as normal behavior; where the classroom to prison

pipeline has yet to be disrupted; and, where conscious people are working hard to try and raise healthy, happy, and whole children. We cannot promote peace abroad if we don't live it at home. I urge you to reconsider your position and remember as one wise sage once said, 'If you want to make the world a better place, take a look at yourself and then make that change!'"

I cannot stop thinking about war and how senseless it is to "fight" for peace and use violence as a way to get to a state of nonviolence. I thought about the only two wars that I believed were completely justified: the Revolutionary War, where we as a nation fought for our independence from British rule; and the Civil War, where the Union fought for the end of American enslavement. Both of these were life and death situations that happened in our country (on our soil) and where violence was the only way that the other side would retreat and that true change would come.

I feel as if the world is falling down around me and that I am not doing enough to keep it upright. I woke up this morning and I looked at my hands because in my dreams I had blood on them that I could not wash off, no matter how hard I tried. I realized after I settled back down on my bed that when my President chooses to go to war, my elected officials support him, and my fellow citizens execute his orders, then my hands like theirs are bloody. I am just as responsible. When I do not speak up and speak out then I am teaching you to act as sheep, blindly following wherever their leaders will take them. I think of leaders like Hitler, Jim Jones, Robert Mugabe, Kim Jong II, and Idi Amin Dada, men who abused their power and were directly responsible for the deaths of thousands of people and I realize that I must be the change. I must be the change. I must be the change that I want to see in the world and I must model the type of change that I want you to embrace and to one day become. And once I am the change, then I must teach you to be the change.

Boys, to be clear: I am not naive. I know that violence is a part of the world that we live in but I will never ever believe that war is an answer for anything, particularly in this case. Although the Bible refers to us as sheep, we do not have to blindly follow our government. We can question their policies. We can hold them accountable. We can be conscientious objectors…perhaps if more individuals around the world stand up and speak out, we can force our leaders to think through their decisions. I sometimes wonder if making a decision to go to war would be more difficult for our leaders if it meant that they would have to be on the front line. So, in the midst of all of the ongoing conversations about war and violence and destruction, what can I leave you…well I can start with this poem:

You are the sons of life's longing for itself
(for Kofi and Amir, ©2013)

If I allow you to spend most of your hours playing violent video games, how can I expect for you to spend the rest of your time working for peace and justice?

If I allow you to engage in unhealthy activities that contradict and interrupt the healthy activities you should be involved in, how can I expect you to be able to create a better world?

If I never tell you no or teach you about peace and love, how can I expect you to be patient and to work to make the world better for others?

If I teach you that your talents were given to you to make your lives better, how can I expect you to understand that "given" means "entrusted" and your job is to use your talents to make the world better?

If I condone violence in any form and allow you to take pleasure in video games where satisfaction and points are tied to the number of people you kill, how can I ever expect you to see all people as extended members of our family and not as targets?

If I sit back and allow you to wordlessly digest images of sex and violence and torture and inhumanity as easily as you digest your peas and corn then shouldn't be held responsible for the actions that happened as a result of the seeds I have planted?

I look forward to the day when peace happens, peace is embraced, and peace defines who we are.

*****

My dear sweet boys, these are the lessons that I believe that all parents should be teaching their children: that peace is possible and should start at home, war and violence are never answers to conflict, and as global citizens, we must work together to be the type of change that we want to see in this world.

on preserving history[10]

August 29, 2013

In 2006, when Barack Obama first ran for president, I was an enthusiastic supporter. I campaigned for him, spoke at community centers, visited homes and used the very tiny platform that I had to sing his praises. Even though I had started the year as a Hillary Clinton supporter, I was captivated (as were many others) and hopeful that the election of a black man was going to be the answer to Dr. Martin Luther King, Jr.'s dream. Unlike my Nana who thought he was some type of a Messiah, I did not believe that he could walk on water, heal the sick, end racism, or reduce the national debt by any significant amount. At the same time, I did believe his rhetoric and I thought that change would come. I believed that he was going to be a compassionate leader who would do everything he could to remind us that we are all in this struggle—to make our world a better place—together.

At that time, when I voted for him, I was not just voting for myself. I was voting for all of my ancestors who never saw the end of the American system of enslavement and who died before *Brown v. Board* was decided. I was voting for my grandfather who died before Obama became the Democratic candidate and for my grandmother, Reds, who never had a chance to experience the joy that comes from having a black man sitting at the center of the American political system. I was voting for you and (at least in my mind) to try and right some of the wrongs of the past. I wanted you to have the experience of seeing a black man in the highest office in the land.

The second time he ran, I was a reluctant supporter. I was unimpressed with his first term and I was no longer moved by his rhetoric. My vote for him was actually a vote against his opponent. I still believed in change but I knew from work during his first term that real change takes a very long time and perhaps, in my lifetime, it may never come. As I have borne witness to how his second term has unfolded, I have become more and more jaded about the direction of this country, his true intentions, and the deep rooted feelings of racism that have been brought to light since he first took office. Even though I know that one person, no matter how powerful he is, cannot change the world (I remove people like Jesus Christ, Dr. King, and Gandhi from this equation, as one could easily argue that their actions did indeed change the world.), the president does set the tone for our nation. Every time he makes a public appearance, whether it is at an anti-violence rally in Chicago or at a beer tent in Iowa, it gives us insight into what he thinks are the most important issues at that time. When he focuses his attention on something or someone, the world glances at it, as well.

This was why I was so excited when I heard that President Obama might have been planning to visit the home of Harriet Tubman in Auburn. For the past couple of weeks, due in large part to the release of a sex tape video, her life and her legacy have been discussed throughout the country. With all of the confusion and attention, I thought it was appropriate for him to visit her house at this time. He did not have to meet with the family or make a speech but his presence alone would have spoken volumes.

As it stands now, simply because he chose not to visit (after booking a room close to her home and working out a gym across the street), a statement has been made that her life and her legacy are not that important and can and should be ignored. I am unable to get a read on our president and am often surprised and moved by some of the things that he does and does not do. In this case, I wonder why he chose not to visit and I have spent the last day thinking about it. Perhaps he was concerned about overextending himself; or he felt that those of us who have already spoken up about Harriet Tubman have done an adequate job and his voice was not needed; maybe he ran out of time or his people told him that this was one controversy—coming on the heels of the George Zimmerman verdict—that he should ignore; maybe he does not feel connected to Harriet Tubman since he does not come from a history of American enslavement or maybe he is fed up with the race issue and feels that other people need to carry the torch; maybe he needed to get back home to tend to his new dog or he had a long-standing basketball game appointment that he didn't want to break; or maybe, and this one is the saddest of all, he really does not realize how important the life and legacy of Harriet Tubman are to the world and how connected she is to his wife and his daughters.

I support our president but in this moment, I summarily reject any excuse he may have about not visiting her home. I would suggest that he take a moment and examine history because if people like Harriet Tubman would not have run away or fought for freedom 150 years ago, then folks like my father could not have marched for freedom 50 years ago, and people like me could not have voted for him five years ago. It is all connected, my sons, a very simple circle of life.

on teaching other people's kids

February 15, 2009

Do you remember how unhappy I was from 2005-2007? You once called me a mean mommy. You said that every time I came home, I was mad at you for no reason at all. It was a hard period in my life as I was working as a middle school Advanced Academics Social Studies teacher at West Baltimore Middle School. As a mid-career changer (I had been a television producer and documentary for ten years), I did not really know what to expect when I walked into the classroom. I believed that I would encounter a room full of excited students who wanted to immerse themselves in the study of America. I envisioned two rows of students lined up at my door, dressed in white and blue starched linen dresses and shorts, carrying their writing tablets and instruments, and bringing me red shiny apples. I thought my students would love me and would see me as a fountain of knowledge and wisdom. This was my dream!

Unfortunately, my dream and my reality (which always happens to me) were not in anyway similar to one another. In fact, on the first day of school after fighting to get in the front door of my school, breaking up two hallway brawls, being called at least two of the words on my "Don't Say" list, and accidentally bumping into a student who thought I was trying to frisk him, I realized that not only was this not my dream I actually felt that it was not my life! Those were the most difficult and in many ways, the most fulfilling years of my adult life. I cried almost everyday during that first year. I realized that these students—the ones who were angry at the world and at me—are the future. These students who struggled to understand even the most basic of concepts were one day going to be responsible for deciding the fate of the world.

I remember walking through the cafeteria while the students were forced to have yet another quiet lunch and realizing that I was afraid of the future that they were going to create. I could not understand how these students—who came to a school everyday that had bars on the windows, no doors on the bathroom stalls, no toilet tissue or soap, no vegetables or fresh fruit in the cafeteria, no books in the library or art supplies in the art room, no pencils, paper, or text books–could ever be trusted to create a world that I would want to live in.

I did not blame my students, as they do not have any control over the schools that they must attend, I blamed the system. I blamed the city and in so many ways, I blamed myself. I probably could have and should have done more, though at the time, I thought that I was doing all that I could do. I probably should have stayed instead of going back to get to my Ph.D. and then escaping to the golden tower of academia. I could have and should have done more. If I want them to be able to create a world where I want to live then I must be willing to roll up my sleeves and work with them and for them to make their world (the one that I am currently creating) better for them.

My life was full of contradictions because even though I taught in the Advanced Academics program (there were 120 students in the program and 70% of them are currently attending college), I worked in a school where most of the students were neither advanced nor interested in pursuing their academics. I remember when I was selected to receive the 2006 Maryland History Teacher of the Year Award, I was both happy and sad: happy because my Advanced Academic students were smart and confident and fully capable of carving out a life for themselves (because being smart and being recognized for being smart meant that they would have choices and opportunities); and I was sad because as hard as I worked for my 120 students, I did very little for the other 900 students in the school who were reading below grade level and were not prepared to attend either a college-prep or a technical school.

In Baltimore City, by the time a student is finished with the first semester of their eighth grade year, they will know whether or not college is a viable goal. Since their high school acceptance is based upon their seventh grade test scores and the grades from seventh grade and the first semester of eighth grade, if they did not do well then they will not be accepted into either a city wide (college prep) or technical high school. The only choice left for them is to attend their neighborhood (zone) school, where very few, if any of the students, go on to attend college. These are the students who scared me the most because by the time that they became eighth graders, they knew that they were going to have very few opportunities to get the skills they would need to be successful in this world.

Even though I left, I think often of all of my fellow teachers who stayed behind to make sure that no child is left behind. This poem is for them and to them:

We See You
(for Mrs. McNeill and Mrs. Kinney, ©2006)

Teaching in the inner city is not for the gentle-hearted:

it is not for those who need constant gratitude, extrinsic rewards or pats on the back

it is not for those who want to do something else.

It is not a job for the light-hearted:

for those who never see the light at the end of the tunnel or the peak at the top of the mountain;

for those who do not love other children almost as much as they love their own.

People who teach are different from those who have been called to teach our children:

the ones who have been labeled, left behind, looked over, forgotten, abused and disregarded

the ones who live in communities where motherhood at 16 is a celebration and jail time by 20 is a rite of passage.

Our children and those who have been called to teach them are the special ones;

They are the ones who are responsible for teaching our children not only how to speak but how to speak up and speak out.

Those who are called to teach inner city children are wired to wear and they can't help but teach somebody something even when nobody is volunteering to learn.

They never get lost in a sea of unchecked papers, have never met a child they couldn't teach, a lesson plan they couldn't write, a challenge they couldn't meet or an administrator they couldn't tame.

They are professionals and can admit the system's mistakes, own up to their own failures and state very clearly how it used to be, what it could be, and how it should be when it comes to educating our children.

These teachers are real and are uncluttered by the need for recognition instead preferring to do it right simply because it needs to be done…right.

They choose to teach on the edge of discovery…where creative ideas and our children tend to be.

Their work in its simplest form is sharing knowledge and giving back to the children that everybody usually takes from.

They are grounded, well planted oak trees whose branches are made up of the children that they have taught, saved and loved.

They guide our children safely from the sunset of learning to the sunrise of new beginnings.

Over time, we have learned that teaching our children and training them are two different things…those who are wired have found a way to do both.

nurturing masculinity

March 17, 2013

Kofi:

I watched you earlier this evening at your first boy/girl mixer, as you were walking around with your hands in your pocket looking a little confused and unsure. I saw the girl that you like and I saw you follow her around the gym; looking for opportunities to say something to her, finding ways to touch her arm or grab her hand. I saw you try to dance with her and how the two of you, slightly embarrassed, decided to call it off, and to just stand and talk instead. I saw the way you stood when other boys came over and tried to get her attention. I saw the protective shrug of your shoulders as if you were staking claim, letting them know that this space was your space. You did not know it at the time but my eyes never left you. You were growing up right before my eyes. In so many ways, you are still my little baby boy who needs to be fed and carried, changed and comforted. You are my firstborn and everything I learned about being a mommy, I learned from practicing on you.

As I watched you, I realized that you are on your way to becoming the man—the person—that I had always hoped you would become. I have done (and will continue to do) everything that I can to nurture you. You once asked me what a feminist looked like and I–partly in jest—stated that if I have done my job right, you would see a feminist every time you look in the mirror. I laughed when I said it but later, after I had had a moment to reflect, I realized how much truth there was in that statement. I am raising you to believe in and defend political, economic, and social rights for women. At the same time, I am also raising you as a Christian. For some this may seem like a contradiction but for me, I cannot imagine sending you out into the world without having deep roots in both of these areas. My hope is that this grounding and teaching will help you as you decide how you are going to see the world and your place in it.

As you and your friend made your way around the gym, talking and laughing at jokes only the two of you could hear, I realized that you were at the beginning of a dating ritual that goes back much farther than you or I and will now be a part of your life up until you get married. I do want to caution you because it quite possible that she will break your heart. I say that not because I want your heart to be broken, but because I know that you are only twelve. You have a long way to go before you really understand what it means to fall in love and to commit your life to just one person. You are at the beginning and in so many ways; the beginning is really a good place to be. As you stand here, at the threshold of your unknown, I wanted to offer you some relationship advice that I hope will act as a compass to help you navigate yourself through this well-worn journey:

1. Be kind to her and treat her well. Just like you, she has parents who love her and believe in her. She is your equal, not your property, so give her the space to speak her mind and the ability to change yours. Treat her with as much dignity and respect as you treat me.

2. Make her laugh and enjoy laughing with her. There is nothing more comforting than being around someone you

can laugh with. Laughter is both a balm and a healing salve. Trust me, as you get older, there will be days when laughing will keep you from walking out of the door or from saying something that you can never take back.

3. Guard your heart and guard hers. You have been raised well and have been treated well. You know what it is like to be appreciated and supported and loved. Do not expect, accept, or offer to her anything less than that.

4. Be nice to her mother. Even though mothers are not perfect, some of us work very hard to give our children choices. We sacrifice over and over again to give you the best that we can afford. We try to raise you in such a way that you will have more victories than defeats, more friends than enemies, and more opportunities than regrets and after we have done all of that, we realize that all we have left is the ability to pray our heads off and hope for the best. Treat her mother as you would like for her to treat me.

5. Get the door for her, pull out her chair, and pay for everything on the first date (and I am smiling as I write this). I know that these are old-fashioned values and that they probably go against everything I have done/said to raise you as a feminist; but, there is still something in me that enjoys those things. I call it two-sided feminism and I struggle with it everyday. I know that you know that women are equal and that we can get our own doors, pull out our own chairs, and pay our own way but I must admit to you how nice it is to come across a guy who cares enough for you to want to do those things for you.

6. Resist the temptation to make her your entire world. Although there may be days when you feel like the sun rises and sets only on her, it does not. As special as she may be, she is still just a part of your life and not your life.

Furthermore, do not allow her to make you her world for heavy is the burden of being the only one responsible for making someone happy.

7. Be as honest as possible with her and with yourself, as there is nothing more painful than ambiguity from someone you think you like and who you think feels the same way. If you do not like here, then let her down easily and let her go. Allow her to move forward to find someone who will adore and cherish her.

8. Be a person of your word and if you say you are going to call or be there or do something, then just get it done.

9. Be good to yourself and be good to her. Even though this is probably not the girl that you are going to marry, you still want to leave her with fond memories of you. Your grandfather used to tell us to leave people better than when we found them, to not pull them down, or intentionally hurt them. You want to pull her up and build her up. You want to make her feel that she is visible and that she is important.

10. Be patient with her, with your relationship, and with yourself. Love takes a long time to grow. It must be nurtured and tended to and sometimes it must be left alone. You cannot rush the process nor should you have to.

11. Do not settle for anyone other than the best person that God has for you. Your father and I are pouring everything we have into you because we love you and we see your potential. In our eyes, you are a diamond and we are responsible for brushing off the dirt to help you to shine. It is not always easy for you to see your own potential or to believe that you are special but, in those moments when you cannot believe in yourself, believe in us because we believe in you. Sometimes, just knowing

that someone believes in you will help you to make it through the darkest of days, the loneliest of nights, and to make the best decision.

12. Put God first. I saved this one for last because this is the foundation that everything else must be built upon. You are being raised in a Christian home and it is a part of who you are. As you make decisions about "who" to date and "when" to date and sometimes even "why" to date—my prayer is that you filter all of these questions through the lens that your father and I have given you. (I know that like me you will come to a point where you will make a decision about what you believe and about whether you want to live your life as a Christian—when you get to that point, know that I will be there with an open heart, a supportive word, and a patient spirit to either advise you or support you in whatever decision you make). My hope is that Christ is involved in every decision that you make. So, if you want to ask her out, I hope you pray about it. If you want a second date, then I hope you pray about it. If you want to ask her to marry you (or she has asked you to marry her) then I (really) hope you pray about it. And then, when you get married, I hope that like your father and I, the two of you start praying about everything—together.

You, my dear sweet son, are at the beginning and even if I wanted to, I cannot protect your heart from getting broken. All I can do is love you, support you, and do my best to help guide your ship into its port. The road will be long, but with good guidance and a lot of prayer, then you and your brother will find the ones that are meant for you.

integritas

February 28, 2013

Boys, on the night before I spoke at the White House, I sat down in my closet (and yes, when you get married and have kids you will have a closet, where you can sit and not be bothered) and realized that in five years, I will be 50 years old. Me, I will be one half of a century. I grabbed my little compact and a flashlight and looked at myself in the mirror, for a long time. I kept saying in five years, you will be fifty. In five years, you will be fifty. I looked at every wrinkle, pulled at some of my grey hairs and realized that I was ready. I had been preparing to be fifty all of my life because when I was growing up, all the cool sistas that I knew were all over fifty. I was born in rural South Carolina, a state that was the first to decide to secede from the Union rather than recognize black people as citizen, as equals. My father moved us to Washington, DC. We were a family of six. Your grandfather, as a Baptist minister, was very active in the Civil Rights Movement and he used to spoon feed us stories of justice and equality with our peas and our corn at every meal. He saw race in everything and early on, so did I. As we got older he taught us to be like Sankofa birds—to fly forward but to always have our heads turned backwards: in other words the future is what we will claim and the past reminds us that we have what we need to claim it.

I participated in my first protest march when I was thirteen years old. We were visiting South Carolina (we spent every summer there) and there was a small store that sat on the corner by Nana's house. The storeowner, an older white man who did not like black people, had framed several "For Whites Only" signs and had posted them all over the walls. The first time my sister and I walked into the shop, he pointed at the sign and then told us to leave. Well! I ran home, took out a piece of paper and wrote "Freedom Yesterday, Freedom Today, and Freedom Tomorrow." (My father had just told us about George Wallace who once uttered the famous line "Segregation now. Segregation tomorrow. Segregation forever"). When Nana saw me marching outside the store, back and forth with my little sign, she stopped her car, and told me to get in. On the way home, she told me the story of Emmett Till and she said that power will never ever concede without a struggle and that I needed to make sure that when I chose to struggle I was prepared for the consequences.

She said that I did not have to be old to know what the right thing was to do. She once heard Dick Gregory speak and he talked about a four-year-old boy who had been arrested and held in prison for four days. When he was released, the reporters asked him what he wanted and he said, "I want my teetum, I want my teetum." He could not even say the word freedom. He just knew what he wanted. I learned a very valuable lesson that night and I committed myself to fighting for what I believed was right.

But, in many ways, growing up in the Washington, DC as the daughter of a pastor meant that I did not struggle half as much as I would have liked. My life, as I remember it, was not really about confronting struggle, it was about confronting and overcoming the microagressions that black people and women have to deal with everyday—the little things that pick at our spirit and try to destroy our souls. I come from a long line of strong black women and even though I tried to be like Sankofa, it was becoming increasingly difficult for me to look back and fly forward. My life was my own to shape and to mold so I started looking forward and flying forward and I gave myself permission to try and fail, to fall in love and to get my heart broken. I gave myself permission to be the person that I had always wanted to be. So what I have learned and what do I want to leave you? If I had to sum up my life in one word—it would be "Integritas."

I once read a story that said that during the time of the Roman Army, right before the soldiers went into the battle, the General would line them up and inspect them one by one. He would check their battle armor, their weapons, and their eyes. He was looking for any sign of weakness, hesitation, or fear. In the end, if he felt that they were ready to do battle, he would pat them on the chest and say, "Integritas," which meant that they had integrity. They were sound, unimpaired, and in perfect condition. They were ready for battle and hungry for victory! I believe that we are in the midst of a war, a war to confront and dismantle the systemic racism, classism, and sexism that are so prevalent in our society. I need to make sure that you are ready and that you are armed with the knowledge of our past, a clear understanding of our present, and a plan for our future. Integritas! That is one of your main weapons. You must be sound, unimpaired, and in perfect condition to be vigilant. You must be focused on being the best of who we are. Your future, your destiny, and your goals belong to you.

I believe that learning how to live with Integritas is similar to learning how to live like an African balboa tree. Your grandfather taught me many years ago that as a child activist and a pastor, I needed to live like a balboa tree. It took me many years of living like a palm tree, where I bent and swayed for everyone and everything; a walnut tree, where I supplied nutrients for everyone else without keeping some for myself; and, for a short time, as a pine tree, where I learned how to live in conditions and environments that were hostile and detrimental to my health and well-being before I learned to live as a balboa tree, never bending, never swaying, properly rooted and well nurtured:

I. I had to start by understanding the strength of my roots. We are the descendants of enslaved men and women who chose to survive, despite the incredible odds that they had faced and were facing everyday. They chose, similar in many ways to the mates on Peter's ship, to hang onto the broken pieces. Our roots are the things that stabilize us, nurture us, and anchor us. Our roots are long-lived and give us insight into who you are and what you can become.

II. I learned that I needed both the sun and the rain to grow. We live our lives everyday hoping that the good times, the moments when we are peaceful and happy, will never end. And when they do, we find it hard to move forward. I have had some very difficult moments, we all have. Moments when I thought I could not go on but yet I did. I had to learn how to laugh again, how to sleep through the night, and how not to live in fear that something might happen. I had to learn, in some cases, how to be me all over again. But I did it. I weathered the storm and though the sun has come out again, I am now more prepared for the rainy days and more appreciative of the sunnier ones.

III. I learned how to work my limbs. The Franciscan Cross goes in two different directions, both up and out. The bottom part of the Strike- has two hands laying across one another, moving in two different directions. It means that as we reach up to God, we should also reach out to each other. Our hands, like the limbs of a tree, should then reach both up and out. Our hands, as extensions of our hearts, should be used to serve and to help. Susan Taylor once said that, "Hands that serve are holier than lips that pray." It is not enough to speak about the change we wish to see in the world. We must be the change, live the change, and enact the change that we want to see. We do not come into this life nor do we go through it alone. It is the people in our lives who form us and shape us into who we are. We are not meant to do this alone. It is too hard. Imagine if you will, never having anyone to talk to or laugh with, argue with, or cry with. Life is messy. It is unpredictable and it usually does not make much sense. In a nation ripe with iPads, cell phones, private schools, Ivy League colleges, and Martha's Vineyard vacations, it is hard to believe that there are some people in this country whose daily reality is similar to the lives of those who live in developing countries. They live beyond the sphere of your understanding. They are temporarily experiencing homelessness, suffering without health care, and living below the poverty line. The government makes political decisions about their lives without having a true understanding of how they live. This is where you come in. Those of us who are able and stable must find ways to serve and to do it consistently with passion and compassion. We must reach up to what we believe in and whom we serve and reach out to those who walk beside us so that we can become true servants. We have to work our limbs both up and out.

IV. I had to learn that Balboa trees do not move around. They stand tall, constantly becoming more than what they used to be. It is inspirational in so many ways. You should want to be the kind of person who does their job and does it well all of the time. You should want to inspire others by being the best of who you are, at all times. You should want to grow more into who you are supposed to be, better than you were yesterday but not as good as you are going to be tomorrow.

V. Finally, I had to learn how to fall. Before lumberjacks chop down a tree, they slowly walk around it so that they can determine in what direction the tree will fall. Trees, like us, will fall. The only difference is that unlike them, we can get back up. You need to understand and accept that you will fall and you will probably fall often. I believe that this is what separates the good from the great. I am fairly certain that Harriet Tubman was not the first enslaved woman to "free" herself but she was the only one who committed herself to going back time and time again to free others. Picasso was not the only painter who could have painted the Sistine Chapel but his work and his vision is what transformed the original design from a painting of the twelve apostles into a masterpiece with more than 300 different figures. The great ones fall and do so over and over again and each and every time, no matter the cost, they get back up. You need to learn how to fall and to do it in such a way that you can position yourself to get back up again. In so many ways, this is just as important as talent and opportunity because this is what determines your character and what puts you in a position to be great.

The problems that we are facing as a nation and as a race are not there because of something that we did. These are inherited problems. We inherited racism, we inherited sexism, and we have inherited classism. It is now a part of us. It defines us and in so many ways, it limits us. We are a nation that is stained with the sticky remnants of enslavement and though we have tried, we cannot seem to move beyond it. It took African Americans roughly 208 years to become legally free; another 84 years before the back of Jim Crow was broken; and, another 54 years after that before Americans elected a black president. Change takes time.

Integritas means that we are prepared to do battle, without fear and without hesitation. I am teaching you how to be committed to justice, equality, and change. Commit yourselves to Integritas. Be challenged to be better. Be inspired to be great. Be the change that you want to see and the change that you think can and should come. It is about living with integrity and embodying a spirit of Integritas.

#YourLivesMatter

raising black boys, individually & collectively

i. we must talk frankly about race[11]

August 17, 2014

I would like to write you a love letter about peace and post-racial living, of a wonderful time when all people move freely, of a place where black bodies are not endangered and black life is not criminalized. But that is not your story, and it is not your reality.

As much as I try, I cannot hide my frustration about what happened to Michael Brown in Ferguson, Mo., my disgust over what happened to Eric Garner in Staten Island, N.Y., my outrage over what happened to John Crawford III in Ohio, and my horror over what happened to Ezell Ford in Los Angeles, Calif. —tragic events that have happened within the last month, four unarmed black men killed by police. These are the types of stories that I told you about when you were younger and we talked about the Civil Rights Movement. For some reason, the two of you thought (like I did when I was a child) that I was making these stories up about police officers—using tear gas and water hoses, dogs and chokeholds—to frighten you into behaving. It has taken years for you to realize that these events did happened and it has taken the past month for you to finally accept that these events are still happening.

There are days when being black in America overwhelms me

and makes me want to spend the day in bed/ and times when being a black mother of black boys in America makes me wish I had enough money to move them somewhere anywhere where I could keep them safe from everything. My heart always skips a beat when a cop's car is behind me while I am driving at night, and though you are not old enough to drive, I am already frightened by the day when you are stopped for the crime of driving while black. I have tried to teach you to follow the rules and to respect authority but lately it seems as if the rules are constantly changing and we are always one step behind.

I spent the last week watching as the situation unfolded in Ferguson. I read the minute-by-minute accounts on Twitter and Facebook, as pictures were posted, comments were shared, and tensions escalated. Although many of the facts are still coming to light, there are some things that are undisputed: Michael Brown was unarmed, he was shot and killed by a police officer whose name was not immediately released, the community responded, and the police (over)reacted.

You wanted to know why some members of the community were breaking windows and looting the stores in their own community, and I shared with you the long-term effects that rioting and looting had on Watts in 1965 and on South Central Los Angeles in 1992. I had and still have no answers for what it must be like to be so frustrated and to feel so disempowered that the only way that you think that you can express yourself is to destroy your own community. I closed my eyes and tried to imagine what it must be like to feel as if the very breath that sustains you was being taken from you daily and that the only way that you could respond, the only way that you could make the world see your suffering, the only way that you could reclaim your breath, was to tear down everything that your hands could touch. I was not surprised when Ferguson exploded nor when I saw the video footage showing tear gas, stun grenades, a LRAD Sound Cannon and smoke bombs. I feel as if I have become a pessimist because I believe that this is what happens when you combine racial profiling, racism, community frustration and police brutality.

I had hoped that President Barack Obama, instead of telling us that it was time to heal, would have instead used his powerful platform to encourage the nation to finally have a serious conversation about race. He could have used that moment, when the entire world was watching and waiting, to talk to us about how important it is for us to share our feelings of anger, fear, rage and frustration. I am not suggesting that the president should host another feel-good session, where a few representatives meet at the White House, have tea, and talk about how we are now post-racial because we no longer "see" race. I am talking about doing the hard work: sitting down in small diverse community groups and wrestling with the questions of how race and our feelings about it are still dividing our country. We need to ask ourselves what type of society we want to live in, what type of world we are willing to leave to our children, and what we are willing to do to be the type of change that we believe needs to happen in the world. We must be willing to express our feelings, to open up and make ourselves vulnerable, to be held accountable for what we say and do and to commit ourselves to doing more and to being better.

I am not surprised that Ferguson exploded, the police overreacted, and that communities around the country, including in Baltimore, responded by having a national moment of silence in memory of Michael Brown. I am surprised that we do not realize that it is time to have a conversation about race and that this conversation must take place before we begin the process of healing and before something else happens to capture the nation's attention.

ii. killing/saving/loving black boys

August 19, 2014

The more I thought about what happened in Ferguson the more frustrated I have become. Today, I am not sure if I can protect you. So instead I will write and cry and pray.

Killing/Saving/Loving Black Boys
(for Kofi and Amir, ©2014)

I would like to write you a love letter about peace/ of a time when black men, like black panthers, roamed free/ of a place where black bodies were not endangered and black life was not criminalized.

Alas, I am not old enough to remember life back that far (if it ever even existed in this country).

Neither am I old enough to remember life before *Brown*.

I suspect (though) that it was not much different than it is now in places like Ferguson and New York and Florida/ places across America where the crime of breathing while black is still punishable by death.

I used to be afraid of white sheets (wouldn't even use them on my bed) 'till folks traded them in for blue uniforms/ and then traded them in for billy clubs.

My heart always skips a beat when a cop's car is behind me while I'm driving at night/ and though you are not old enough to drive, I am already frightened by the day when you are stopped for the crime of driving while black.

There are days when being black in America overwhelms me and makes me want to spend the day in bed/ and times when being the black mother of a black boys in America makes me wish I had enough money to move you somewhere where I could keep you safe.

Safe from them—the ones who see your life as expendable and unnecessary/ and from us—those who look at you without realizing that you are a mirror that simply reflects them.

I often think about slavery and how different life was when you could see the hand that held the chain that was attached to the ball that was tied to your ankle.

We come from a people who experienced this daily and still chose to survive.

Survival is our legacy.

And since we survived the Middle Passage as involuntary passengers on a trip that sealed our fate/ And we survived slavery, whips and lashes by learning how to give way and stay small/ And we survived the Civil War by claiming freedom at the hands of those who looked like our oppressors

—surviving is our goal.

We are a long-willed stubborn people.

Who survived sharecropping and the period called the nadir,

The Great Depression, Vietnam, Reaganomics, and crack cocaine.

We are a stubborn and strong-willed people.

Who survived lynchings, cross burnings, and being terrorized for wanting to vote and for trying to reclaim our voices.

We who have been beaten and starved,

Disenfranchised and disempowered,

Overlooked and ignored,

Underpaid and underrepresented.

But

We survived because we are strong-willed and stubborn.

And though there are times when we are like strangers in a foreign land/ we look around and wonder how we got here/ we take stock and realize how little we actually have/ we wonder how long we will continue to suffer and die at the hands of both the oppressor and of the oppressed

—we survive anyway.

Because survival is our legacy.

There are days when I look at the two of you and my heart swells with pride

As I think about all that you use to be and all that you can become,

And then I stop and catch my breath/ I grab my chest and clutch my pearls/

I blink back tears and shake my head/ for I am sure that the mother of every unarmed black boy who has died kneeling at the feet of a racist system where guilty verdicts are meted out

—one chokehold at a time

—one gunshot at a time

—one lynching at a time

—one whipping at a time.

I think of them daily (what black mother of black boys doesn't)

I try to speak their names/ going back as far as I can remember/ adding new names daily.

I do it so that I can remember/ so that the two of you can't forget/ so that together we can add their names and their lives to the wind so that a piece of them and this moment will remain at this place/ even though we will move on.

There are nights when I stand in the doorway of your room--not to wake up you up for the revolution but to simply remind myself that, just for a moment, you are still safe and still here.

All I want (at this moment) is what every other mother wants around the world—the simple comfort of knowing that the lives of my sons do matter and that my work—to pour love, light, and truth into them, will not be in vain.

I move from being upset and hurt to being angry and infuriated: because from skittles to hoodies, loud rap music to cigarillos, toy guns to iced tea; whether you are 18 or 12(!), college bound or not, a homeboy or a choir boy, hands held up or down on your knees, walking in the street or standing in Wal-Mart, during the day or at night, in Ohio or in Florida or in Baltimore ~ you two are Not SAFE in this country.

As your very angry mother, I cannot and will not rest until that truth/that sad reality has been changed.

We are survivors.

We are stubborn.

We are strong-willed.

Survival is our legacy and surviving everyday—in this system—is our goal.

There will come a day when you will know what it means to be free/what it means to be safe/what is means to just be.

I look forward to being there with you, on the dawn of this new day, and to celebrating with you.

we who believe in the freedom canNOT rest (or #BlackLivesMatter)[12]

November 1, 2014

#BlackLivesMatter: boys no matter what they tell you, you are important, you are special, you are here for a reason, and you have work to do. If you ever forget who you are, just ask me and I will remind you. I promise you, with everything that is good in me that I will never forget.

I. Sweet Honey in the Rock

My favorite moments with you happened when you were small children. I used to sit with you in your room and play music by Sweet Honey in the Rock. You used to sing with me as we danced around the room, shaking our heads, and clapping our hands. I remember one day when I was singing the words to "Ella's Song" and I started to cry. We were sitting in your room and you came up to me and grabbed my hands and wanted to know why Mommy was crying and singing. I put you on my lap and just held you tight because I knew that in so many ways the words to that song had to be my rallying cry. I was the mother of young black warriors and if I believed in freedom and if I wanted the day to come when the "killing of black men (black mother's sons) was as important as the killing of white men (white mother's sons)," then I, as an activist and a mother, could not rest.[13] I had to use everything that I had (all of my talent, my time, and my energy) to help create a world where you could grow up and be free. Your father and I have done all that we can for you and your brother and yet, in so many of the ways that are important, we have failed you.

II. The Killing of Black Children: Yesterday, Today, & Tomorrow

I have spent the last few days thinking about Trayvon Martin, Emmett Till, the Four Little Girls, Michael Brown, Eric Garner, the children of MOVE, and the thousands of nameless faceless children who were/are the victims of the senseless violence that grew (and grows) from the roots of racism. I have cried and yelled, prayed and mediated, and then I did what I do best and that is simply grabbed my pen and wrote. When I think back to the Zimmerman case, I must admit that up until the moment that the verdict was read, I still believed that justice would it be served. I followed the case as closely as I could and I did my best to explain it to you while trying to protect you from it. I read all of the articles and listened closely to the testimony. I tried to understand George Zimmerman's version of the truth and tried to look past both the "Knock Knock" joke and the lack of diversity amongst the jurors. I defended the witnesses and even though I felt that some of them were not properly prepared, I believed that the jurors would be able to look past all of the "errors" and see the truth. I remember when I first heard about Trayvon Martin and George Zimmerman and about what had happened on that night. I was outraged to find that on the night that Zimmerman shot Martin, he was quickly released from custody. When he was finally arrested and charges were filed, I breathed a long sigh of relief. I called your grandfather and he reminded me about how black people over the years have been and are severely disappointed by the judicial system. He felt that justice would not be served and that we would find ourselves back at the beginning of the struggle, yet again. I heard him but I chose to believe. We are Americans and though this country has let us down so many times, I still believe in it and I still believe that we are going to get beyond race and become the country that I have always believed that we could be. We got through the Revolution, slavery, Jim Crow, and the suffrage movement, and someday we will get past this thing called race. I thought that we would get past it before you grew up but I was wrong.

III. A Mother and Her Child

At this moment, I am writing to the two of you because I am hurting and I am scared. In the past couple of months, our nation has changed and is changing so quickly that I feel that all I can do is just tread water. I write to you tonight because young men who look like you are dying at alarming rates, some at the hands of white vigilantes and some (too many really) at the hands of other black men. I write to you because I fear that I have not properly prepared you to do the type of battle that you are going to have to do to make the world better for your children, my future grandchildren. I am writing to you because I am trying to find the words to apologize for being a part of the generation that has failed you. We have dropped the baton and have not done our part to make this world a better place.

We made you believe that you were the center of the universe and have therefore not prepared you for battle. I remember the first time that you (my dear sweet oldest son) swung the bat in T-ball and hit the ball out past second base. You were so excited that you ran around the bases, twice. I shouted and screamed and Daddy carried you on his shoulders. We celebrated your first home run with milkshakes and a special dinner. We called everyone we knew and told them about your amazing home run. We were so excited that we convinced you that every time you swung the bat, you would hit a home run.

IV. Baseball as a Metaphor for Life

As life would have it, at the next game when you came up to bat, you kept swinging but you could not hit the ball. You were devastated and we had a hard time explaining to you that we were wrong because every swing was not going to result in a home run. We were unable to convince you and for the rest of the season, you kept expecting to hit a home run and you were incredibly disappointed when you did not. As you have grown up over the years, we have tried so hard to teach you that life is not measured in home runs but in getting back up to bat again. We were talking about baseball but also about life. You will strike out and you have to learn how to move past it, put it behind you, and pick the bat up over and over again. I have shared all of my home runs with you but I have shielded you from my strikeouts. Today I wish I would have shown you every rejection letter rather than the published, polished articles or shared with you how disappointed I was when I was rejected rather than how elated I felt to be accepted. I told you all about how happy I was when I pledged Delta Sigma Theta but I never mentioned how hard it was when I was rejected the first time I applied and all of my friends pledged without me. You were there when I spoke at the White House for the Black History Month panel but I never told you how nervous I was every single moment of every single day that I would not say the "right" thing. You see me walk around with my head held high but you do not know how often your grandfather—when I was teenager—had to grab my chin, lift my head, look me in the eye and remind me of how special I was. You always smile when your Daddy tells me how much how much he loves me but you do not know how many times I have heard those words from men who did not love me or, in some cases, did not even like me. You attend an independent school but you are not aware (though I am and your grandfather is) of how long it took before schools like that accepted boys and girls who look like you. You are not prepared to do battle because I have tried so hard to convince you (and myself) that every battle had been fought and had been won.

V. Freedom's Song

My sons, I am a child of someone who participated in the Civil Rights Movement (and freedom and resistance are a part of your legacy) and I have had some incredible shoes to fill. I grew up listening to the stories and benefitting from the work, but I (and those who grew up with me) never experienced separate water fountains or being forced to sit in the back of the bus. I grew up seeing people who looked like me in positions of power. Your grandfather committed his whole life to helping to create a world where despite the color of my skin, my gender, or my economic standing, no door would ever be closed to me. He was part of the nameless faceless masses who marched behind King and sat down at lunch counters, boycotted public transportation, sang and prayed and hoped for changed, was arrested and held overnight in prison cells, and was called the n-word more times than they would like to remember. And despite all of the odds against him, he helped to change the world. He loved going to school because the teachers (all of them black and female) would tell him that the only way that the world was going to change was by him choosing to be a change agent. He had big dreams and he knew that the only way to make those dreams come true was to fight and sacrifice over and over again. He made a vow that his children would never have to experience life like he did, and we did not.

I was sent abroad for the first time when I was in the sixth grade. I attended an advanced academics school (they called it a "school without walls") and our class trip was to Canada to see Niagara Falls. I remember sitting in class one day when my classmates who sat by the window yelled out that my daddy was there and was getting out of a white car wearing a white suit. They said that he looked like a pimp, to me he looked like my knight in shining armor. He came upstairs and paid for my $600 trip in cash. I remember because he paid in five and ten dollar bills. Your grandfather used to own a gas station and used to work the night shift so instead of going to the bank to make his morning deposit, he came to my school to pay for my trip. I have never believed that any door was ever closed to me. I was my father's daughter and I understood that I was benefitting from his work. I was able to live the life that he had always dreamed about. I knew that he struggled. I knew that he sacrificed. I knew that I was not entitled to these rewards but that my father had earned them for me and was giving them to me.

VI. Going Forward From Here

When you were growing up, I did not share these stories with you on a regular basis. I never made you learn the words to "We Shall Overcome" or "Lift Every Voice and Sing" though your grandfather made me learn both before I turned ten. Although I talked to you over and over again about the struggle, I never made it real to you. I never explained to you that the past is the present and that you are still under attack and under suspicion because of the color of your skin. You have been raised in a privileged environment, have traveled extensively, and have met people from all over the world. You have no idea of what it means to struggle.

You have never been made to feel invisible and have never felt profiled or threatened. I have tried to protect you when I should have prepared you. Beloved, you are strong and smart, brilliant and funny. You are the next generation and the blood of every one of our brave and courageous ancestors flows through you. Now that things in Ferguson are starting to calm down and we are now looking for solutions to these age old problems, your father and I will turn our attention to speaking to you and your brother everyday about what you need to know and what you need to do to navigate your way through this world. The world will be a better place and the two of you will help to create it and where I (and those of my generation) have failed, your generation must and will succeed.

(finally) having that talk about race[14]

July 20, 2013

For the past couple of months, your father and I have been talking about what lessons we wanted to teach you now that you are on the verge of becoming a teenager and your life is changing in so many ways. We thought that we would talk about love and relationships, friendships and heartbreaks, dreaming and working towards your dream. Our plans changed after the Zimmerman verdict was released. We realized that it was time to have the "talk" with you and your brother. Although both of you are familiar with the events that happened during the Civil Rights Movement, we do not believe that you are as well versed about current racial issues as you need to be. In some households, "the talk" is about sex, abstinence, protection, pregnancy, and making good decisions. In our household, "the talk" is about race relations, the perceived criminality of black men and boys, gang and drug violence, and the unwritten crime of walking and breathing while black. For us the talk is about keeping you safe, getting you home at night, and making sure you are always where you are supposed to be.

When you were little boys, whenever you started crying, we would put you in your car seats and take you for a drive through downtown Baltimore. We would play Sweet Honey in the Rock and sing out loud until you started moving your head, clapping your hands, and singing along. You grew up on folk music and freedom songs, and though you did not understand them, we had always hoped that the meaning of the words would someday make sense. We vowed, as all parents do, to protect you and to do all that we could to make the world a better and safer place, where you could grow up and be free.

We have done all that we can for both of you, and yet, in so many of the ways that are important, we have failed you. The world is not a better place. It is not safer, and people are not equal. We are still being judged (and judging others) by the color of their skin rather than the content of their character. We have not gotten to the Promised Land and are really starting to question whether that land actually exists.

We are the parents of two African-American boys, and every day that we leave the house, we know that we could become Trayvon Martin's parents.

We are aware of how difficult it is to raise an African American boy in this city and in this country. We are familiar with the stereotypes and the racial profiling and have read and studied cases where young, black men are always assumed to be guilty and then must prove their innocence. We know that gun homicide is the leading cause of death of African-American males between ages 15-19. Your father and your grandfather have experienced more times than they would like to admit what it means to be reminded that you are black and male—and therefore you are dangerous and criminal.

I cried when the George Zimmerman verdict was announced, but those tears are nothing compared to the ones that I shed over the senseless violence that happens every day across this city. Even though Baltimore does not have a written "stand your ground" law, we do have unwritten "ground standing" laws in the inner city that define masculinity and respect in relation to how black boys treat and respond to one another.

Fortunately, you are not familiar with either of those laws. Up until this point, you have been shielded and protected from gang violence, overzealous vigilantes, impoverished communities, drugs and substandard schools. We had hoped that with the election of a black president and a young, black, female mayor, and by keeping you in protected environments, we could avoid having "the talk." We thought that we could "achieve" our way out of the talk by providing you with opportunity after opportunity to travel and learn and just experience the world.

After the Zimmerman verdict, and after reading about the increase in violent deaths this year across Baltimore City, we knew that "the talk" was long overdue and for us, it was telling you how to act when you get stopped by a police officer or what to do when you are followed in a store, or even how to respond when aggressive behavior starts happening on the neighborhood playground.

For 12 years, you have been protected. You have no idea of what it means to struggle. You have never been made to feel invisible and have never felt profiled or threatened. We have protected you when we probably should have prepared you. Now that the jury has spoken and the dust has settled, we will turn our attention to speaking to you and your brother every day about what you need to know and what you need to do to navigate your way through this city and through this country. We still believe that the world will be a better place and that the changes that we are hoping for can be accomplished by you.

a never-ending war[15]

February 17, 2014

In the days leading up to the end of the Michael Dunn "loud music" case—in which a white Florida man shot and killed a 17-year-old black teen after getting into an argument over the boy's so-called "thug" music—I was overwhelmed with feelings of restlessness, worry, frustration and fear.

They were the same feelings I had at the end of the George Zimmerman trial. The same ones I have when I think about the day when you will be old enough to drive or walk to the store by yourselves. I worry so much about what could happen to you simply because you are black and male. I feel like your father and I are in the midst of this never-ending war, the same war that my parents and my grandparents fought. It is the same war that black people have been fighting in this country since American slavery was first legalized. This war is simply to keep you safe in a society that devalues you, suspects you, fears you, and often dismisses you. It is a war that I now fear I am losing.

When you were first born, we held you in our arms and promised you that we would love and protect you. When you learned how to crawl, we ran around the house moving things out of your way. When you learned how to toddle, we walked behind you, always ready to catch you right before you fell. When you started school, we used to check in with your teachers every day to make sure that you were comfortable and safe and happy. We taught you how to say please and thank you, how to raise your hands in school before you spoke and how to wait your turn. We taught you to be respectful and polite. We spent hours reading to and with you, taking you to the library, to the museums and to see Shakespeare in the Park. We saved our money, moved into a safe neighborhood and sacrificed so that you could attend the best schools, take piano, and play sports. We took you to church and made sure that you learned your scriptures and prayed before you ate your food. We really believed that we were doing everything that we could do to keep you safe, to beat the odds, and to win this war. There was a moment when Barack Obama was first elected president that I thought that the war had finally ended and that we had won. We celebrated because we believed that the work that had been done to create a fair and just society. We believed that America was finally colorblind and post racial. We have come to realize that we were wrong.

We are still living in a country where you will be judged by the color of your skin and not the content of your character. I believe that it does not matter how much education you have or how polite you are or how much money we make or that you can play the piano and fence and swim. In this country, no matter where you are or what you are doing, you will still be seen as threats and thugs and criminals. You will be seen as disposable.

My heart broke last year, when the Zimmerman verdict was read and I wondered aloud if it was open season on black boys. Your father and I had our race talk with you and talked to you about what it means to be perceived as a criminal even if you are just walking down the street. We told you what to do when you were approached by the cops or were followed in a store. At the same time, I quietly asked myself, over and over again, how many more weaponless black boys were going to die as a result of white men standing their ground. Do you remember how you followed the Dunn case very closely, asking questions about the defense and about the law? You argued with each other and with me because you believe that this is a human rights issue and that no person has the right to shoot into a car full of people. We sat and listened to the outcome and tried to understand how the jury failed to reach a verdict on the murder charge against Dunn, convicting him only of three counts of second-degree attempted murder. You (my sweet youngest boy) wanted to know if we would ever live in a society where boys like Jordan Davis, Dunn's victim; Trayvon Martin; or Emmett Till would ever have justice. You (my older and wiser son) wanted to know that in addition to not being able to wear a hoodie or stand on a corner or ride on the subway, does this mean that you can never sit in a car with your friends and play music. Although I am helping you to understand that these issues are much more complicated than that, in so many ways I do recognize that they are not. We live in a society where black boys are not able to walk free and where they are devalued and are without personhood. We are living in a society where the war continues. Your father and I are doing all we can to prepare you to fight this war. We believe that you are the ones we have been waiting for, the ones who will end this war, the ones who will bring about peace.

black paintings on the wall

October 1, 2013

When you were four years old (and your brother was three), we visited the Reginald F. Lewis Museum of Maryland African American History and Culture. The Museum had just opened and we had been selected as the "focus family," so a reporter from The Baltimore Sun followed you around and captured your excitement about experiencing black history for the first time. I remember that later that day you told me that you were proud to be black because being black meant something big. You said, "I'm going to do great things because I come from great people." During that time, we made frequent trips down to the Museum and you became familiar with every exhibit, statute, and painting. I used to take the two of you to the third floor, find a quiet corner, pull out an African American picture book, and we would sit there and read. You used to take your sketchbooks and would sit on the floor and pretend to copy a painting or a sculpture. We would sit down in front of these amazing quilts and I would tell you stories about how black history is a part of the American quilt and though we have had some very difficult times in this country, we are still a part of its fabric and our blood is mixed with the soil. I told you that you were the descendants of black men and women who chose to survive and in doing so they stood tall in the face of uncertainty, fear, and unchecked violence.

You loved being at the Museum and I loved that you were surrounded by images of people who did great things who looked like you and who were all from Maryland. I wanted you to fall in love with black history so that you could begin to develop a healthy and positive black racial identity. I knew that when you started school and started studying American history more formally, you would be offered a slightly different interpretation of black history. People that looked like you would only be talked about in February and the lessons would only include the names and experiences of those who are often talked about during this time. I knew that when you were in your classrooms, you would not learn about the life of Robert M. Bell or Frances Ellen Watkins Harper; Vivien Thomas or Daniel Alexander Payne Murray; Cab Calloway or Billie Holiday, all Marylanders. I knew that you would only get this type of exposure and this type of learning from the Lewis Museum and you did.

You are now as adapt and comfortable talking about the richness of black history as you are with talking about white history. You do not see yourselves as outsiders because you know you are descended from a community of people whose contributions are stitched into the fabric of our nation. I remember the first time you saw Judge Robert M. Bell in person and you both said, "It's him. It's the man whose robe hangs in the Museum!" To you, Judge Bell was a hero and not just because of his contributions and his accomplishments but because his picture and his robe hung in the Lewis Museum—a place that celebrates and recognizes greatness. The years that you spent growing up in the Museum and learning about Maryland African American history firsthand have had a significant impact on your lives. And now, at twelve and ten, you are smart and talented and you are comfortable with who you are and clear about who you are becoming. We visited the Museum two weeks ago and as you walked though there, confident and self-assured, I could not help but give thanks that there was a place here in Maryland where you could go and see what you could become. You laughed as you walked through, remembering the days you spent running through those hallowed halls. Kofi, you said that the Museum was like holy ground because over the years, it has served as a reminder of the beauty, the importance, the significance, and the richness of Maryland's African American history.

My heart leaped that day because I knew that no matter where your life would take you, your knowledge of the richness of your culture would always be with you.

bending the arc of change[16]

December 15, 2014

Boys:

Earlier this month, we attended the Ferguson in Baltimore Teach-In at Red Emma's Bookstore Coffeehouse. It was your first meeting for social justice and equality. You sat quietly while I spoke, taking notes and shaking your head in agreement to what I was saying. I watched the two of you as you moved through the audience, stopping and listening to conversations, making connections and introducing yourselves. I was proud of you. You asked me later about Dr. King and the moral arc because you did not understand why I kept referencing or how it connected to Ferguson.

In 1853, Unitarian minister and abolitionist Theodore Parker said that he did not understand the arc of the moral universe, and though it was long, he was sure that it was bending toward justice. In a speech in Montgomery, Ala., 112 years later, Rev. Martin Luther King, when asked about how long it would take to see social justice, responded that it would not take long because the arc of the moral universe was bending toward justice.

It has been almost 50 years since then, and with everything

that has happened over the past four months—from the deaths of Michael Brown and Eric Garner to the grand jury decisions not to indict the officers who killed them—it feels as if the arc is still bending and justice is taking a long time to get here. Protests (both violent and peaceful) have erupted in major cities across the country, including Baltimore. It is a racially diverse movement that is uniting people in ways that have not been seen since the civil rights movement.

As you know, I have spent the semester teaching about Ferguson in my classroom. My students wanted to know what they could do to be a part of the change that they believed was happening around the country. I told them they should focus on changing themselves and their communities. I had them spend some time examining and confronting their own racial biases. I taught them about the social construction of race and class and assigned follow-up readings to help guide our discussions. I taught them how to facilitate difficult and emotional (but necessary) conversations about race and class. I told them that years from now, they will not remember the tests that I gave them or the parties they attended, but they will remember that this was a time when they actively grabbed the reins of democracy and worked to bend the arc closer to justice.

The ongoing protests, in so many ways, are no longer about the incidents that happened in Ferguson or in Staten Island, N.Y. They speak to larger issues around the ongoing treatment and criminalization of unarmed black males and females and the ways in which some police officers abuse their authoritative power without accountability.

We do not live (nor do we want to) in a police state. We live in a democracy, which means that we have a government that is for the people and not a government that is designed to control the people. We are standing here at the crossroads of freedom and equality during a year when we are celebrating and commemorating American history moments—from the 1964 Civil Rights Act to King's Nobel Peace Prize. It is an interesting time because the arc that King and Parker talked about, the one that has been dormant for so long, is now being bent once again, even though it may not be bending as quickly as we would like.

During this time of historic anniversaries, we have seen what it means to have a grand jury make decisions that the rest of the country either cannot or will not accept. We have witnessed the repeated disappointment that some communities feel when our president does not adequately address their hurt and pain. It is almost as if he does not understand how tiring and frustrating it is to have to prove to people, everyday, that #BlackLivesMatter.

When we yell and say that "We Can't Breathe," we are saying that we feel as if the American political and social system is doing all that it can to squeeze the very life out of us. "We Can't Breathe" means that we are tired of the stress that comes from breathing while black in this country. "We Can't Breathe" means that we want the system to see us and to respect us. "We Can't Breathe," when yelled by a diverse group of American citizens, means that we recognize that this country was built by and belongs to all of us.

We are in the midst of a social movement, and those of us who know the racial and economic history of our country must be charged with the responsibility of teaching it so that we do not repeat it. Boys, the arc of the moral universe is long, but together, we can finally and completely bend it all the way to justice.

re/creation

The two of you once asked me how much did I love you...

Completeness...
(for Kofi and Amir, ©2007)

...let all little boys someday
be re/created just like you
gentle caring souls
with yesterday's freedom songs
hidden in the arch of your backs
in the depth of your laughs
with pierced sharp features
outlining the essence
of sunburnt brown ageless faces
with tireless energy
a thirst for knowledge
an insatiable curiosity
seeking out tomorrow's mountains
to climb like warriors
with ebony ashen faces

and wind-song voices
young soldiers who will learn over time
how to bend yesterday's struggles
for a hope starved race
of people

kofi & amir,
if there were no little boys like you
to love & worry about & care for
to play with & imagine with & laugh with
on lazy afternoons, busy workdays
and make believe vacations
little boys like you
who have learned how to smile
once I have dried your tears
patched up your bruises
and repaired your dreams
without little boys like you
to struggle for, to slay dragons for, to blaze a path for
little boys, who are learning how to love
and learning how to fly
whose very presence makes me think of
of places where sunburnt people
aren't three piece stilted
and nine to five suited
of another time where black panthers & black boys
roamed free
without little boys like you
there would be no reason for me to struggle
no reason to dream/no reason to grow

in the dawn of a brand new day

(the one that poets and dreamers
are talking about)
the one that's sure to come

let all little boys be re/created like you
learn all about you
and how you are being nurtured and raised
by a strong willed woman
who gave up everything
to be your mommy
and found herself
  - exactly where she always wanted to be

let them know who you are
so that they can understand
why everyday without fail
I give thanks, praying silently,
for just having two little black boys
 who have ended my silence
and transformed my space
two little boys, like you, in my life.

(Endnotes)

1. "Nikki-Rosa." http://www.poetryfoundation.org/poem/177827; I am grateful to my students in my F'2013 CM330 Stereotypes course who finally helped me to put some text around this idea. I have been wrestling for years with trying to figure out what is needed to help a person move from one income level to the next —in the words of my students it's "the little extras."

2. My title comes from Audre Lorde's book, "The Cancer Journals" (1980), that details her battle with breast cancer. In the spirit of anonymity, when I first wrote this I decided to use gender neutral terms when I described my dear sweet loved one (my hope was that when they saw themselves in my story, they would be encouraged).

3. This article was originally published in The Baltimore Sun under the title of "My Heart Just Stopped: Remembering Maya Angelou." May 31, 2014 http://articles.baltimoresun.com/2014-05-31/news/bs-edan-gelou-20140531_1_martin-luther-king-jr-caged-bird-sings-maya-angelou (Accessed 28 June 2014); For more on Maya Angelou and her impact as a writer, see Kim Pearson's Blog Post " What I learned from meeting Maya Angelou: There's always something wanting to come." http://kimpearson.net/?p=1984 (Accessed 28 May 2014).

4. Toni Cade Bambara was an author and a documentary filmmaker who passed away on December 9, 1995; Nelson Mandela was the first black President of South Africa and passed away at the age of 95 on December 5, 2013; President John F. Kennedy was assassinated in Dallas, Texas on November 22 1963; Martin Luther King, Jr. was assassinated on April 4, 1968 at the Lorraine Motel in Atlanta, Georgia; Medgar Evers was assassinated outside of his home on June 12, 1963 in Jackson, Mississippi; and the Four Little Girls—Addie Mae Collins, Cynthia Wesley, Carole Robertson, and Denise McNair—were killed in the bombing of the16th Street Baptist Church in Birmingham, Alabama on September 15, 1963.

5. In 1961, Robert Frost spoke at the inauguration of President John F. Kennedy, becoming the first poet to speak at a presidential inauguration; Maya Angelou, "On the Pulse of the Morning." Inaugural Poem. January 20, 1993. http://poetry.eserver.org/angelou.html (Accessed 28 June 2014).

6. Maya Angelou, *I Know Why the Caged Bird Sings*, (New York: Random House: 1969).

7. Maya Angelou, "Still I Rise," http://www.poets.org/poetsorg/poem/still-i-rise (Accessed 27 June 2014)

8. David McCullough, Jr. "2012 Wellesley High School Commencement Address," https://www.youtube.com/watch?v=_lfxYhtf8o4 (Accessed January 5, 2014); McCullough, *You Are Not Special And Other Encouragements.* (New York: Ecco, 2014)

9. A version of this letter was published in The Baltimore Sun on September 17, 2014 http://www.baltimoresun.com/news/opinion/oped/bs-ed-syria-20130908-story.html#ixzz2eMDuEDZs

10. A version of this letter was published on August 27, 2013 on syracuse.

com.

11. A version of this letter was published in <u>The Baltimore Sun</u> on August 17, 2014 <u>http://articles.baltimoresun.com/2014-08-17/news/bs-ed-ferguson-20140817_1_civil-rights-movement-police-officer-love-letter</u> (Accessed 7 January 2015).

12. <u>http://blacklivesmatter.com/</u> (Accessed 7 January 2015).

13. Sweet Honey in the Rock, "Ella's Song," <u>http://www.google.com/url?sa=t&rct=j&q=&esrc=s&source=web&cd=1&ved=0CCIQyCkwAA&url=http%3A%2F%2Fwww.youtube.com%2Fwatch%3Fv%3DU6Uus--gFrc&ei=txOyVLLGNMGxggTmqYGACg&usg=AFQjCNEKRSXGmOdx08G6_K21pyWdYKkw8w&sig2=38OwiOhZbSubTeNnK3_NpQ&bvm=bv.83339334,d.eXY</u> (Accessed 7 January 2015).

14. A version of this letter was published in <u>The Baltimore Sun</u> on July 21, 2013 under the title "After Trayvon: Having the 'talk' With Our Son" <u>http://articles.baltimoresun.com/2013-07-21/news/bs-ed-black-youth-20130721_1_trayvon-martin-george-zimmerman-gang-violence</u> (Accessed 7 January 2015).

15. A version of this letter was published in <u>The Baltimore Sun</u> on February 18, 2014 <u>http://articles.baltimoresun.com/2014-02-18/news/bs-ed-dunn-verdict-20140217_1_ending-war-george-zimmerman-sons</u> (Accessed 7 January 2015).

16. A version of this letter was published in <u>The Baltimore Sun</u> on December 16, 2014 <u>http://www.baltimoresun.com/news/opinion/oped/bs-ed-justice-arc-20141216-story.html</u> (Accessed 7 January 2015).

Apprentice House is the country's only campus-based, student-staffed book publishing company. Directed by professors and industry professionals, it is a nonprofit activity of the Communication Department at Loyola University Maryland.

Using state-of-the-art technology and an experiential learning model of education, Apprentice House publishes books in untraditional ways. This dual responsibility as publishers and educators creates an unprecedented collaborative environment among faculty and students, while teaching tomorrow's editors, designers, and marketers.

Outside of class, progress on book projects is carried forth by the AH Book Publishing Club, a co-curricular campus organization supported by Loyola University Maryland's Office of Student Activities.

Eclectic and provocative, Apprentice House titles intend to entertain as well as spark dialogue on a variety of topics. Financial contributions to sustain the press's work are welcomed. Contributions are tax deductible to the fullest extent allowed by the IRS.

To learn more about Apprentice House books or to obtain submission guidelines, please visit www.apprenticehouse.com.

Apprentice House
Communication Department
Loyola University Maryland
4501 N. Charles Street
Baltimore, MD 21210
Ph: 410-617-5265 • Fax: 410-617-2198
info@apprenticehouse.com • www.apprenticehouse.com

CPSIA information can be obtained
at www.ICGtesting.com
Printed in the USA
FFOW03n0927300915
17308FF